WOM

Europe, Migration and Professionalization

Jean Williams

PETER LANG

Bern • Berlin • Bruxelles • Frankfurt am Main • New York • Oxford • Wien

Bibliographic information published by die Deutsche Nationalbibliothek
Die Deutsche Nationalbibliothek lists this publication in the Deutsche
Nationalbibliografie; detailed bibliographic data is available on the Internet
at ‹http://dnb.d-nb.de›.

British Library Cataloguing-in-Publication Data: A catalogue record for this book
is available from The British Library, Great Britain

Library of Congress Cataloging-in-Publication Data

Williams, Jean, 1964-
Globalising women's football : Europe, migration and professionalization / Jean
Williams.
p. cm. – (Savoirs sportifs-sports knowledge, vol.5)
Includes bibliographical references and index.
ISBN 978-3-0343-1315-5
1. Soccer for women–Europe–History. 2. Women soccer players–Europe–History.
3. Women soccer players–Europe–Social conditions. 4. Women soccer players–
Europe–Interviews. I. Title.
GV944.5.W55 2013
796.334082094–dc23
                              2013022616

This book is based on the research project "Women's football, Europe and
professionalisation, 1971–2011" by Dr Jean Williams, financed by the 2010/11
edition of the UEFA Research Grant Programme. The publication of this book
was made possible thanks to additional support from UEFA. The content of this
book is the work of the author alone and does not necessarily represent the
views of UEFA opinion.

ISBN 978-3-0343-1315-5 pb.   ISBN 978-3-0352-0205-2 eBook
ISSN 1663-4616 pb.   ISSN 2235-753X eBook

© Peter Lang AG, International Academic Publishers, Bern 2013
Hochfeldstrasse 32, CH-3012 Bern, Switzerland
info@peterlang.com, www.peterlang.com

To Simon, with thanks for your support and patience.

Table of contents

Abbreviations and Acronyms

AFC	Asian Football Confederation
AIAW	Association for Intercollegiate Athletics for Women
ALFA	Asian Ladies Football Association
CAF	Confédération Africaine de Football
CFA	People's Republic of China Football Association
China '91	FIFA Women's World Championship 1991
CONCACAF	Confederation of North, Central American and Caribbean Association Football
CONMEBOL	Confederación Sudamericana de Fútbol
DFB	Deutscher Fussball-Bund (German Football Association)
ECSC	European Coal and Steel Community
EC	European Community
EU	European Union
FA	Football Association (English)
FAI	Football Association of Ireland
FAW	Football Association of Wales
FAWPL	Football Association Women's Premier League
FFF	Fédération Française de Football (French Football Association)
FICF	Federazione Italiana Calcio Femminile

FIEFF	Fédération Internationale Européenne de Football Féminin
FFIGC	Federazione Femminile Italiana Gioco Calcio
FIFA	Fédération Internationale de Football Association
FIFA U17 WC	FIFA Under Seventeen World Championship for Men
FIFA U17 WWC	FIFA Under Seventeen World Cup for Women
FIFA U19 WWC	FIFA Under Nineteen World Cup for Women
FIFA U20 WWC	FIFA Under Twenty World Cup for Women
FSFI	Fédération Sportive Féminine Internationale
FSFSF	Fédération des Sociétés Féminines Sportives de France
IOC	International Olympic Committee
ISF	International Sports Federation
LFAI	Ladies Football Association of Ireland
Korea DPR	Democratic People's Republic of Korea (North Korea)
Korea Republic	Republic of Korea (South Korea)
NOC	National Olympic Committee
OFC	Oceania Football Confederation
PFA	Professional Footballers' Association
SEA	Single European Act
SFA	Scottish Football Association
SWFA	Scottish Women's Football Association

UEFA	Union des Associations Européennes de Football
USSF	United States Soccer Federation
WNBA	Women's National Basketball Association
WSL	FA Women's Super League
WUSA	Women's United Soccer Association
WPS	Women's Professional Soccer League
WWC '99	Women's World Cup 1999
WWC '03	Women's World Cup 2003
WWC '07	Women's World Cup 2007
WWC '11	Women's World Cup 2011

Introduction: Europe, Patterns of Migration and the Professionalization of Women's Football

How should a history of Europe be configured? This should not be a simple collection of individual national stories. This is not the only, or perhaps even the best way, to attempt to trace a process of European historical development...In the context of sport, Lanfranchi and Taylor's study of the patterns of professional footballer migration serves as a guide on how to break away from a national fixation...What is Europe? How is it represented to us? To what extent do we feel European? Our notion of «Europe» must be seen in terms of these various issues, and not as territory constructed with western-Eurocentric vision (Hill 2010: 1).

1. Post-war Europe and the rise of women's football

When, in 1951, six European states formed the European Coal and Steel Community (ECSC), via the Treaty of Paris, economic integration on the continent accelerated. The ensuing Treaty of Rome, signed in 1957 by Belgium, France rance, Germany, Italy, Luxembourg and the Netherlands, began to merge some areas of fiscal policy. More than fifty years later, over thirty states have become involved in a complex arrangement of political, social and cultural ties in the European Union (EU). However, there have been significant exceptions. Cold War politics particularly affected central and eastern regions (Edelman 1993: 5-10). While federalists before the war described a possible union including the USSR, communist government in the countries of central and eastern Europe saw a Soviet «sphere of influence» become, in Churchill's words, an «iron curtain» by March 1946 (Kowalski and Porter 1997: 100-21). The subsequent recommencement of the civil war in Greece, territorial demands on Turkey and claims on Persia then combined with the exit of the Soviet representative from the Four-Power Council of Foreign Ministers in 1947. From this point on, the division of Germany into a Federal Republic (West Germany) and the Democratic Republic (East Germany) determined different notions of

European-identity until the fall of the Berlin Wall and the reunification of the country in October 1990. Across Europe, diplomacy and policy «faced» East or West, although, as a recent exhibition at the V&A Museum in London indicated, social, political, economic and cultural influences crossed physical and ideological divides (V&A 2009). Since 1990 a number of new European states have become independent; marking a growth in the size and intricacy of migration across the region as a whole.

While sport, identity and representation are therefore central to this study, a detailed assessment of changing political systems in Europe since 1945 is beyond its scope[1]. One academic approach to the subject of the EU has tended to emphasize the role of political parties in power at a given time (inter-governmentalism). However, from its antecedents before the Second World War, the EU was conceptualised as having a much wider and more powerful role (supranationalism). From this scholarly perspective, the union, its institutions and activities are treated as a progressively autonomous body. The first expansion of what was the European Community (EC) in 1973, with the accession of Denmark, Britain and Ireland, was part of a growth about which many people remain ambivalent. Britain's previous application to join had been vetoed by French President de Gaulle in 1963; Norway had applied to join the EC in June 1970 but voters rejected the idea in a referendum held in 1972 and both countries remain, by and large, Euro-sceptic. Extending the EC to Greece, Portugal and Spain involved protracted negotiations. The Mediterranean enlargements were eventually agreed in 1979 in the case of Greece, and 1985 for Portugal and Spain (coming into force in 1981 and 1986 respectively).

Subsequent regional conflicts and economic difficulty have made further augmentation of the EU's role a relatively slow and precarious affair. Nevertheless, in this increasing sense of Europeanization, the four most significant aspects debated in the public domain have been federalism, a widening and deepening of the union and a degree of flexible integration. These are worth outlining briefly because the same processes can be said to be, more or less, present in the changing Europeanisation of football over the same period. Federalism involved nation-states entering various forms of partnership involving supranational organization. Widening the EU has also been contentious. The current membership of twenty-seven states has been scheduled to expand further still, in spite of acute economic circum-

1   Appendix 1 summarizes the necessary context of the expansion of the European Union
    since the ECSC agreement to the present (European Commission 2010).

stances across the region. EU candidate countries at the time of writing include Croatia; The former Yugoslav Republic of Macedonia; Turkey and Iceland. In addition, potential candidate countries include Albania, Bosnia and Herzegovina, Kosovo under UN Security Council Resolution 1244, Montenegro and Serbia. Some European nations are deeply committed to the European Union and others remain less so. Consequently, the extent to which the EU has spoken on behalf of European nations as an umbrella organization at various points in its history remains debatable. The degree of flexible integration has meant that individual nations have sometimes been able to advance their domestic interests through the EU, but this is another challenging topic beyond the scope of what concerns us here.

While most academics would acknowledge that a changing sense of Europe has been significant for sport, the opening quotation from Jeff Hill shows that it is only recently that it has been conceptualized with any rigour. Compared with the amount of ink spilt on the topic of monetary union and the common currency from 1999, or opinion polls that show a commitment to federalism, sport has been relatively neglected (George and Bache 2001: 1). Perhaps the current enthusiasm for European football competition, such as the annual Champions' League trophy, can be seen as evidence of a relatively banal indicator of European-identity. When a Chelsea supporter wears her team shirt to attend a Champions' League match in Barcelona, a sense of being European might be less evident than other characteristics, including local pride. Greater connectivity, such as improved transport and communication networks, make football as much a creative-cultural industry, as a sport. Switzerland, home to important governing bodies for the sport, remains more Euro-sceptic than other countries but has a prominent place in the history of world football over the same period. It is as well not to presume too much of a confluence of interest, therefore: fundamental values which appear to be highlighted both by the EU and football, such as peace, non-discrimination, solidarity, unity and sustainable development, can be somewhat nebulous in their application, in spite of the apparent consensus of their use.

Nevertheless, the EU has sought to become more involved in the business of sport as the twentieth century progressed. The European Parliament declared 1992 Olympic Year and by 1999 the Helsinki Report established that the sport industry required supranational regulation. The relationship with Olympism has since further been formalized with a permanent European Olympic Committee (EOC). The *White Paper on Sport* issued in

2007 went further to argue that health, social inclusion, education, competition law, freedom of movement, criminal liability and the protection of minors all came under the umbrella of EU. However, there are clear limits to a sense of European identity in sport. Proposals to create a European team whose athletes would wear a national and EU symbol while participating in the Olympic Games have been resisted.

In football, independent and autonomous national associations usually wish to tolerate intervention only when European-wide interests are concerned (Lanfranchi and Taylor 2001: 5). As one of the most well-known EU mottos would have it, most football national associations prefer to show «Unity in Diversity» rather than through a wider sense of European-ness. Until the late 1990s, for example, newly-formed associations affiliated first to of the Federation Internationale de Football Associations (FIFA), the world-body of football since 1904, then to their continental confederation, though the reverse is now the case. Therefore, the growth of the EU has been just one way of interpreting how a greater sense of Europe has become evident in sporting terms since 1945 (Agergaard and Bothelo 2010: 157).

Arguments linking sporting migration with recent globalization processes may neglect longer historical trends. The commercialization of sport had a significant pre history and, from the nineteenth century onwards, it was allied with other urbanized creative industries. These included large international exhibitions; the music hall and theatre. Each of these business models used similar technologies of enclosing areas of entertainment to which a paying public were admitted. Gentlemen and scholars formed the Football Association in 1863, though there remains debate about how far their codified laws of the game relied upon previous versions of rules (Mason 1980: 34-8). With the significant influence of Sheffield and northern industrial towns, the game was primarily developed and disseminated by business connections; in particular entrepreneurs who understood mass markets for both participants and spectators (Harvey 2005: 10-5). The establishment in England of the FA Cup in 1871 and the Football League in 1888 had shown how local and regional rivalries could be stimulated well before such trophy competitions could be described as national, let alone international in perspective (Taylor 2005: 35-7). Charles Korr's important study of West Ham United illustrated how ambitious teams had to make a difficult choice over whether to remain representative of a local area or draw in playing talent and support in order to compete against the best opposition (1986: 24). Club competition stimulated the migration of players and distinct patterns of diffusion (such as the movement south of Scottish «anglo» professionals) began to emerge at the same time that some destinations became nodes where specific groups of foreign nationals clustered. Consequently, a degree of cultural transfer was allied with athletic labour migration well before the Second World War.

As part of European post-war reconstruction from 1945 onwards, commercial links, player transfers and the exchange of knowledge became more evident and systematized so that England's World Cup victory of 1966 could be celebrated in the form of endorsed musical, mascot and magazine products specific to the tournament (Davies 2004: 50-2). This merchandise opened the sport to consumers well beyond the stadium. The football collectibles market itself became a by-product of the convergence between sporting spectacle, business and the representation of other cultures. As well as new professional characteristics in sport, there were innovative commercial cultures developing out of participatory and elite competition. Education and leisure opportunities spread unevenly across western Europe and new global communication technologies increased a sense of connectivity. Football was a particular beneficiary of these changes. However, regional conflicts, localized practices and individual circumstances also complicated these general trends. This work therefore begins with these multiple and changing aspects of European identity. Rather than a stable meaning, being «European» has implied a fusion, and perhaps some confusion, of terms. Football has meant many things to different people. Neither has professionalism been a straightforward or coherent phenomenon.

A conscious move towards European integration, which was to have wide-ranging and important consequences, coincided in 1951 with an event that seems, on the face of it, isolated, unrelated and insignificant: T. Cranshaw of the Nicaraguan football association wrote to the secretary of FIFA, concerned that he had seen women's football in Costa Rica and knew of almost 20,000 female players in the United States (Eisenberg et al. 2004: 187). Cranshaw enquired what FIFA intended to do about this shocking development. The governing body, based in Switzerland, responded that it had no concern with, or jurisdiction over, women's football. In consequence, it could not offer advice either to Mr Cranshaw or to its affiliated associations on this issue. However, there had been a history of European women's football going back at least to the 1880s and the world-body must have been aware of at least some of this: Jules Rimet, who had been a president of both the French Football Federation (FFF) and FIFA, had assisted in two female Paris-based matches attended by 10,000 spectators in 1920 (Dietschy 2010: 503).

At the time of writing much has changed: football has held a men's World Cup in South Africa in 2010; one of the first African-hosted sporting mega-events. The 2018 edition has been awarded to Russia and the 2022 competition to Qatar; so football is still consciously moving into emerging markets for the sport. Increasing the gender equity profile of football has coincided with these aims. However, the movement of people and expertise in women's football remains a neglected academic topic. The first Women's World Championship was held in PR China in 1991 and the country also hosted the 2007 Women's World Cup (WWC) in a number of key cities. The United States has held two Women's World Cup competitions in 1999 and 2003. Sweden hosted the Women's World Cup in 1995 and an Olympic Games tournament first showcased women's football at Atlanta in 1996. Thereafter, Sydney, Athens and Beijing became important milestones in the cross-cultural transfer of Olympic women's football. FIFA awarded the finals of the Women's World Cup to Germany in 2011, breaking attendance records for a female-only tournament on the continent. This live attendance was surpassed again during the 2012 Olympic Games in London, where over 660,000 people attended women's matches. There are now also two FIFA youth trophies; the U-20 and U-17 Women's World Cup tournaments, held in Germany and Trinidad and Tobago respectively in 2010. The crowded playing schedule includes confederation, regional and national competitions. It is no exaggeration to say that the rise in the number and variety of international fixtures for women players is football's most conspicuous move toward equity in the last twenty-five years. Not only has this changed the way that the sport has been conceptualized, skilled female players have changed the representation of football's technological and institutional networks by moving across the world to play the game.

First, what do we mean by European football and where do women fit into this research agenda? Second, if football is the fastest growing team sport for women, and has had a world tournament since 1991, why has it not become more widespread and commercialised? While research on the international migration of male and female athletes has developed, particularly over the last ten years, we know little about women earning a living from football in various professions and semi professional roles. With an estimated 26 million female players globally, of which 6 million are based in Europe, the evolution of football as a sport and as an industry since 1945 has been dramatic (FIFA 2006: 3). However, there are reasons to be cautious in the optimism that surrounds the growth of the women's game since 1991. The same survey claims only a total of 21 million registered European players, male and female, compared with an educated-guess of 62 million unregistered participants. It is not uncommon to include those who intend to participate in the next year, as well as those who actually do play, for example. Globally today, even by FIFA's own exaggerated figures, women make up ten per cent of the total number of football players at best.

When we look at elites able to earn a living from the game, the disparity is amplified: if there are 60,000 professional players registered in Europe, for example, very few are women. This is striking because the idea of amateurism has, to a large degree, defined what it is to be a professional: under FIFA rules, if a player earns more for their football-playing activity than the expenses that are incurred in performing those duties, they must have a written contract and are thereby considered a professional. While those who do not meet these criteria are considered amateurs, the word professional encompasses a considerable range of activity, from the essentially casual participant supplementing their main income through football, to the multi-millionaire players of Europe's big five leagues in England, France, Germany, Italy and Spain. So, this work asks the following research questions: What are the patterns of movement into, and out of Europe, for paid professional female football players since 1945? How many women and girls are involved in professional careers in European football? How has the growth of female participation since 1945 affected different kinds of professionalization in the football industry? How do European-wide patterns of professional female migration coincide with global markets for women's football?

In order to begin to answer these large topics, it is first of all necessary to consider a brief overview of the growth in European football after 1945. The public profile of the industry has developed massively: issues that were once the concern of a small elite of volunteer directors behind closed doors, are now debated by fans using social media before they have been dignified as little more than rumours. Many authors have pointed out that inter-war competitions were especially significant in providing a platform for post-war developments (Turner and Idorn 2004: 140-1). The European confederation, the Union des Associations Européennes de Football (UEFA), was formed in Switzerland in 1954 with thirty member associations (Albania, Austria, Belgium, Bulgaria, Czechoslovakia, Denmark, England, Finland, France, the Democratic Republic of Germany, the Federal Republic of Germany, Greece, Hungary, Iceland, the Republic of Ireland, Italy, Luxembourg, the Netherlands, Northern Ireland, Norway, Poland, Portugal, Romania, Scotland, Spain, Sweden, Switzerland, the U.S.S.R., Wales and Yugoslavia). UEFA's expansion followed piecemeal as Turkey joined in 1955; Malta in 1960; Cyprus in 1964; Liechtenstein in 1974; San Marino in 1988; the Faroe Islands in 1990; Estonia, Latvia and Lithuania in 1992; Armenia, Belarus, Croatia, Georgia, Slovenia and Ukraine in 1993; Azerbaijan, Israel, Macedonia, Moldova and Slovakia in 1994; Andorra in 1996, Bosnia and Herzegovina in 1998; Kazakhstan in 2002 and Montenegro in 2007. The current membership of UEFA totals fifty-three national associations but this does not represent a neat confluence of political, social and cultural entities. Recent work by De Longevialle has traced the various historical disparities that UEFA attempted to reconcile in its mission to unite Europe through football (2009: 15-20). The membership of specific countries such as Cyprus, Turkey and Israel was problematic, as was the inclusion of micro-states like San Marino or the Faroe Islands and those with contested sovereignty issues, such as Gibraltar.

The flows, patterns and motivations of football's migrants include multiple roles; not just playing and coaching personnel. As a purely administrative body UEFA has grown enormously from an organisation where three people worked full-time in 1960, to a bureaucracy of over 340 employees functioning across multiple languages, borders and cultures. UEFA is an important influencer but also part of a wider trend in the expansion of officialdom: football is now run by its own civil service caricatured by players as «little men in grey suits». As patrician and insular as the replication of such oligarchies have been, world football governance and administration has increased exponentially since the Second World War. The five other FIFA affiliated confederations are: the Asian Football Confederation (AFC) formed in 1954, which currently has forty six national affiliates with its headquarters in Kuala Lumpur, Malaysia; the Confédération Africaine de Football (CAF) founded in 1957, which is comprised of fifty four members and is based in Egypt; the Confederation of North, Central American and Caribbean Association Football (CONCACAF) created in 1961, has forty full associates, (including Guyana, Suriname and French Guyana on the South American continent plus five further associate nations) and is based in New York; the Confederación Sudamericana de Fútbol (CONMEBOL) inaugurated in 1916, presently has ten members and headquarters in Luque, Paraguay and the Oceania Football Confederation (OFC) constituted in 1966, has eleven members at the time of writing with a base in Auckland, New Zealand.

With fifty-three European countries presently affiliated to UEFA, it is an obvious but necessary opening point that the map of football after 1945 has been quite different to the geographical constituency of the EU, with its twenty-seven current members. However, national cultures have rarely been homogenous or static. Transfers of ideas and the movement of people affected football in transnational markets. The «specificity and autonomy» of sport became increasingly contested since the Single European Act (SEA) in 1986. The SEA sought to establish the four basic freedoms of the movement of goods, capital, services, and people within the internal European market. Sport generally, and football in particular, therefore became ever-more subject to EU legislation from the mid 1980s onwards. This was prompted in no small part by the deaths of thirty-nine Juventus FC fans at the Heysel Stadium in Brussels, after they were charged by Liverpool FC supporters before the kick-off of a match between the two teams on the 29 May 1985. The fixture was meant to be a showcase of football on the continent, as Liverpool had won the European Champion Clubs' Cup and Juventus the UEFA Cup Winners' Cup the prior season. The match was controversial for taking place following the deaths, and was decided by a single penalty goal scored by Michel Platini, the current UEFA President, for Juventus. The deaths of three hundred and forty people at a match in the Lenin Stadium between Spartak Moscow and Dutch club Haarlem in October 1982 also became more widely-known amid intense public debate about the roles and responsibilities of national governments in football (Kuper 1994: 39-41). As an important symbolic, social, cultural and economic activity, football came to be seen as an industry requiring a degree of EU regulation. Unsurprisingly, as revenue streams have multiplied, judicial imposition has been strongly resisted by the governing bodies of the sport.

A rather gentlemanly ethos in conducting world sport has given way to trained and professional specialists, alive to the nuance of both business and politics. The executive committee of UEFA had a Commission Committee on the Players' Union and on the Common Market between 1969 and 1991 in order to debate integration issues and to formulate a position for lobbying. Both temporary and permanent migration required multi-disciplinary teams of administrators to enact the necessary transfers. The launch of the English Premiership in 1992 focused increased attention on who was to play in which European league and profoundly changed the economic revenue-sources to the game; most evidently from the media and especially pay to view television. Tournaments are now copyrighted events promoting licensed products that, in the case of men's World Cups, can exceed 500 individual items and sales of US$ 1.5 billion. The complexities of the financial arrangements on this scale can sometimes lead to apocalyptic forecasts for the eventual decline of the game (Giulianotti and Robertson 2009: 95). A decade after Heysel, the «Bosman case» in 1995, involving a Belgian player of that surname, challenged the existence of «quota systems» for the transfer of foreign professionals. The test case showed that no exemption for football would be made if its regulations were held to compromise the individual's rights under EU citizenship laws. While the complexity of the case has been covered in depth elsewhere and is too involved to examine here, EU law has continued to have a world-wide impact on the markets of football.

Europe and its football in 1951, looked very different than their current manifestations[2]. While The Treaty of Lisbon, which entered into force on 1 December 2009, at once consciously modernized the structures of the EU and recognized the «specificity of sport» in article 165, a number of longstanding practices in football remain contested; these include national playing quotas; ticket sales; television rights and perceived monopolies. The President of FIFA, Sepp Blatter has repeatedly addressed the tensions between the role of EU sports ministers and his own powers of regulation (1984, 1995, 2006 and 2010). A distinctly European model of sport and business was discussed between Androulla Vassiliou, the EU Commissioner, and UEFA officials at Nyon in January 2011. As the first visit to UEFA headquarters by a European commissioner with a portfolio for sport, it remains unclear how any outcomes relate to FIFA's position.

---

2   Some key points in the history of European football since the mid-nineteenth century are summarized in Appendix 2, in order to give the required sports-specific background.

The cultural transfer of ideas has been implicit within these processes. As Richard Parrish has shown, this lack of clarity has led to the formation of «advocacy coalitions» involving a mélange comprised of clubs, leagues, governing bodies, lawyers, and the media who promote their common interests by formal and informal means (2003). Brand and Niemann also remind us that academic assessments of football's Europeanisation should be sensitive to transnational, country-specific, regional and localized variants (2007). For instance the German Football Association (DFB) liberalised its nationality restrictions, post-Bosman, beyond the minimum required for EU residents. This effectively expanded the right to earn a living in professional football in Germany, without being considered a foreigner, to all male players living in the member states of UEFA. Of late, diversity has become incorporated into this wider regulatory framework. However, compared with these financially significant and legally complex issues, gender politics has been lower down the scale of football industry priorities. At the same time, global corporations have sought to rebrand and segment football for a variety of distinct demographic groups. We might conclude that, as a sport, football has been more successful in appealing to female consumers than to women players. Unfortunately, due to the constraints of space, the female fan is not considered here, unless she also translated this enthusiasm into a playing career.

Against this general background of the globalized nature of world-wide markets for football, the specific focus of this work is the partial integration of women players and administrators into international and confederation systems, particularly from the early 1970s onwards. Gendered patterns of EU, FIFA and UEFA regulation and development have emerged in this rapidly-changing evolution of football's commercial markets. However, gender has been largely overlooked in considering what constitutes European football and how this has changed over time (Kassimeris 2010). This is all the more striking because multiple aspects of identity such as ethnicity, race, religion, regionalism and so on, have been treated in scholarly work on football since the work of John Bale on cultural geography in 1980. In fact, «identity» is the single most explored topic in the subsequent literature on European football, including recent publications on the media (Crolley and Hand 2006). European sport, particularly football, and its many female forms nevertheless remains to be further developed as an academic specialism (Scraton et al. 1998: 1-27). Consequently, previous accounts of how Europe has been represented, and analyses of a growing

Europeanization in football have often ignored female players, administrators and coaches (Brown 2000: 129-150). While ultimately unsatisfactory as an analysis of gender or football therefore, this body of literature nevertheless provides a convergence of information that has provided an introductory framework for the discussion that follows (Lanfranchi 1994: 163-72).

The inauguration of UEFA's European-wide competition for women's football in 1982 provided national associations with a focus for international comparison. This expanded as more national associations supported representative women's teams and new states sought to develop participation amongst female players. For example, Estonia, Latvia and Lithuania joined UEFA in 1992. For many years, eastern European associations did not have their own budgets as football was integrated across government ministries for health and sport. State systems often did not promote women's football because there was no Women's World Cup until 1991 and no Olympic event until 1996. Since 1992, greater interest in women's football by central European, Balkan and eastern regions has further expanded UEFA's profile and made the map of European football larger. As the first monograph to explore those continent-wide tensions, Appendix 3 summarises the qualitative and quantitative information collected by FIFA and UEFA in relation to national associations, particularly between 1996 and 2003. The text supplements this with research materials from the UEFA and FIFA archives to provide further contextual data.

The movement of female athletes has a long history, whether we consider individual sports, such as pedestrianism and swimming, or team games, such as hockey and football. As highly skilled technicians, female professional sports performers often innovated their own marketplace, either for short or sustained periods of time. Travelling independently, or as part of organized tours, their ideas and practical acumen often bridged sporting, entertainment and artistic networks. Born in 1887, Annette Kellerman was an Australian professional swimmer whose mother was an accomplished musician and father an entrepreneur. Often driven by poverty to attempt dangerous feats, Kellermann moved from performing in glass tanks in Melbourne music halls, to swim the Thames in London. After failing to swim the English Channel three times, she moved to the United States to become a successful film star just as Hollywood began to promote talking films, shot in colour. In contrast, the Preston cotton worker Alice Mills, who played football for the Dick, Kerr Ladies from

1917 until 1923, travelled abroad on sporting tours before moving permanently to the United States in 1924 (Bourke 2000). Football may have introduced Mills to an American way of life but her migration was motivated by much larger patterns of movement from the north of England, as a way of escaping dire local economic circumstances. While she chose to go on a football tour, Alice Mills (and many others like her) were driven to migrate to find work. Women were therefore part of the diffusion and early internationalization of modern sport but individual experience has to be contextualized by the transnational worlds in which women lived. Mills had six children and her American granddaughter would play in the suburban US soccer leagues of the late twentieth century, and write essays at high school about how her «famous» athletic ancestor provided inspiration to take up the sport.

Recent multi-disciplinary work has developed more nuanced approaches to transnational European identities (Taylor 2010: 143-4). The growth of multiethnic national teams has also subsequently changed ideas of sporting representation, for example (Dine and Crosson 2010). A smaller literature has looked at women's football but has focused less on professionalism and migration than on charting national developments (Prudhomme-Poncet 2003). Many see women's increased presence on the international sporting stage as a «recent change» with the women's world cup for cricket set up in 1973, two years before the equivalent men's competition, and with female football and rugby union competitions following in 1991 (Marschik 1998). This work contends that there were connections linking Europe's female football players since the early 1920s that provided a basis for a wider participatory community after World War Two. Although evidence remains fragmentary at best, this awareness of women's football in other countries and cultures helped accelerated transnational growth from the mid 1950s onwards (Carroll 1999, Burke 2005). With more movement came new patterns of migration and conceptions of football (Chang 1981, Brownell 1995). Some of the women who were able to choose to move have been part of the more mobile professions (such as teachers, students, nurses, journalists or lawyers) and others worked in trades with relatively stable practices and good rates of pay (such as the textile, technology and light engineering industries). However, only a small minority of women have been able to earn a full time living in another region or country from football (Beveridge 1975, Begbie 1996). The reasons for this lie in the historical development of football labour markets.

National team selection has been a key element of professionalization for European women football players, both before and after officially-sanctioned competition. National team selection, though not paid work until the twenty-first century in most cases, gave female players a much-increased profile from which they might either extend their careers in football or move to related occupations, such as coaching or the media. The first transnational star of women's football was Michelle Akers, who travelled across her native United States, to Europe and Japan to develop her career. Her celebrity was rapidly exceeded by Mia Hamm, born in 1972, who grew up in a military family based in Italy at a time when women's football was particularly significant in the country (Hamm 1999: 4). After winning the inaugural Women's World Cup with the United States team in 1991, Hamm became so famous by 1999 that the sporting goods brand Nike pitched her as the cultural equivalent of basketball star Michael Jordan in advertisements shown during the Women's World Cup tournament in Los Angeles. She then had the second-largest building on the Nike campus named in her honour and helped to launch a professional league before retiring in 2004 (Hamm 2004: 5). Her eighteen-year career spanned two hundred and twenty five international matches; in which she scored nearly one hundred and sixty goals. An icon, fathers and daughters would wear matching shirts with Hamm's number 9 emblazoned on the back and she set up a foundation after her retirement to promote sport and healthy lifestyles for the young (Chastain 2004: 10). Unlike the women with whom she is often mentioned, such as the Williams sisters and Danica Patrick, Hamm was the first female team player who became a superstar with considerable crossover appeal (Gregg 1999: 5).

In contrast to these American women players, we need to know much more about what Birgit Prinz or Carolina Morace or Kelly Smith represents to their respective fans at home and abroad (Williams 2003: 220). Club and country tensions are also important parts of the story (Williams 2007: 35). More academics are now calling for the attention of researchers to focus on women as being «increasingly enmeshed in the process of making national identity through sport» (Polley 2004). For example, in the context of British women medalists of the Olympic Games, Stephen Wagg suggested that the period 1952 to 1972 saw «a perceptibly different vocabulary» in media promotion of British female athletes (2007: 100-1). What processes are at work in the representation of national women football players? How has the sporting lexicon imagined and depicted the female player?

After considering the research methods and sources used to compile some of the available evidence, individual case studies provide varying examples of professionalism negotiated by some pioneering women players. The changing nature of women's work shows that female football celebrity was also part of the early twentieth century. Industrial welfare schemes included sport and leisure to attract the best workers but there is no evidence that women's football was popularised by such a singular cause during World War One. Not all Dick, Kerr's players worked at the munitions factory of that name and yet the degree of civic recognition they enjoyed as representatives of the firm was considerable (Melling 1998, 1999 and 2001). Transfers to play for the Preston-based team widened from Lancastrians but biographical detail on the team members remains sparse (Russell 1997). By March 1919, Dick, Kerr's of Preston played Newcastle United Ladies at St James Park in front of a crowd of 35,000. Newcastle's striker, Winnie McKenna, already had 130 goals to her name for Vaughan Ladies and signed after the match for Dick, Kerr's though it is unclear for how long. The Dick, Kerr playing personnel was certainly drawn from outside Lancaster and England, with Frenchwoman Louise Ourry (1905-1984) and, later, Scottish player Nancy «The Cannonball» Thomson (1906-2010) moving to Preston and working while they played. Anxieties about how women might change the professional culture of football included cartoons such as «The New Beauty and The Beast» featuring an assertive female player and a deferential male opponent (The Football Favourite, 26 February 1921). Unfortunately, while we have documentary evidence of some aspects of this nascent professionalism, there are few surviving players from this period.

Micro studies looking at the lives of players from the 1960s onwards illustrate a range of professional identities. Meso-professionalism followed, with gradually growing numbers of players and emerging club-level employment for women from the 1980s onwards. Finally, the project considered macro-professionalism, with more widespread international competition in the 1990s and the launch of new semi-professional leagues in the twenty-first century. The concluding comments refer to potential areas of further research. Professional women's football has developed more consistently over the last sixty-year period than at any point previously in the history of the game.

The project has also looked beyond Europe because the United States has some significant influences on how the professional female athlete has been marketed here (Parillo 1999). In the United States model the four main sports (American Football, Baseball, Basketball and Ice Hockey) operate a closed-league system wherein male athletes sell their labour. The number of female high school, college and university football teams expanded rapidly after the enactment of the Title IX amendments in 1972, which stipulated that federally funded education institutions devote equal funding to both sexes (Pauw 1999: 2). The number of female athletes taking part in high school sports multiplied seven times, and soccer had almost a thousand college teams by the turn of the millennium (Whitehead 2007: 15). The aspirational, educated, female soccer player entered the cultural lexicon. Julie Foudy, Mia Hamm's most influential team-mate, turned down a career in medicine at Stanford to play football. Brandi Chastain, Joy Fawcett and Kristine Lilly were also part of this college and university tradition.

An equally significant female professional league in another team sport, The Women's National Basketball Association (WNBA), has now been running for fourteen years (Banet Weiser 1999: 324). It provides one of the most interesting examples of world-wide professional female team-sport migration. The WNBA stretched the playing calendar for basketball by being scheduled in the closed-season of the male populated National Basketball Association (NBA). It also attracted new audiences and innovated sporting-goods merchandise principles with its endorsed mother-and-baby products (Williams 2007: 101). Much of European professional sport, in contrast, operates on models that assume limited commercial viability for women's leagues. Consequently, the launch of closed women's semi-professional football leagues, licensed by the national associations perhaps evidence significant American influence in European football. The next chapter will look at the specifics of this case. For now, having summarized the main themes inherent in the study, the growth of European-wide female football competitions first requires consideration.

2. UEFA, European competitions and the growth of women's football

Seven European countries formed FIFA in 1904: Belgium, Denmark, France, the Netherlands, Spain, Sweden and Switzerland, with Germany intending to join a future agreement. Motivated by a desire to recognise only one national association per state in representative competition, the broader processes of football's cultural transfer had already been begun by club competition and tours (Eisenberg et al. 2004: 58-68). The British were considered to have joined the following year; Slavia Prague effectively represented the Czech football association; Italy and Hungary comprised the tenth and eleventh members. An Olympic football competition was held in London in 1908 hosted by the English FA. At the 1912 Stockholm Olympic Games FIFA first held an international tournament under its own control and the ninety thousand spectators made evident the financial benefits of such a competition. By the First World War, both amateur and professional football had their own commercial markets whether this was for the game itself; including related industries such as the media, gambling and clothing or for more general sporting goods.

The first example of international women's football is difficult to specify but it was probably an unofficial game played under at least under some FA rules in 1881 (Glasgow Herald, 9 may 1881). Evidence of women's football can also be traced back to folk and courtly forms. These include a Song Dynasty (960–1279) three-day contest, where a women's squad composed of one hundred and fifty three members, all in elaborate costume, played with embroidered balls to the accompaniment of a musical band (Williams 2007: 11). After codification, more fixtures were arranged, for example, between teams calling themselves Scotland and England, who played in Edinburgh in 1881. Opposition was widespread but the English Hopewell sisters, Mabel, Maude and Minnie, deserve their place in football's hall of fame as pioneers. Nevertheless the Scottish players were far superior, winning by three goals to nil. The British Ladies Football Club, formed in London in 1895, combined the talents of middle-class Nettie Honeyball as player-secretary with the non-playing president, Lady Florence Dixie. Most of the nineteenth century women enthusiasts enjoyed playing and did what they had to do to participate. Honeyball, Mrs Graham and «Tommy» of the British Ladies Football Club briefly became stars until 1897, when little is then known of their lives. While there is emerging evidence of women's teams in the next twenty years; female football then received transnational impetus from the gymnasium movement in France and from the changing nature of women's work in Britain to become popular to an unprecedented degree.

The term Munitionettes football has been used to describe British women playing matches in front of crowds of up 55,000 in aid of charity between 1917 and 1921 (Brennan 2007). This is something of a misnomer in two senses. Firstly, once the Eastern front had collapsed, the demand for munitions decreased and demobilisation began before the Armistice in November 1918. The most famous team, Dick, Kerr Ladies had begun to play seriously in October 1917 based at the Strand Road tram building and light railway works, originally founded by W. B. Dick and John Kerr of Kilmarnock (Newsham 1998). The team would play more in peacetime than during hostilities, therefore. Regional pride had, of course, been developing for a much longer period with a music hall song commemorating Preston North End as first champions of both the Football League and of the FA Challenge Cup in 1889.

Secondly, there were other work-based women's teams such as Horrockses' Ladies, of the mill owned by the family known as the Cotton Kings of Preston, and Atalanta, an affiliation of professional women, such as teachers and nurses. The Lancashire United Transport Company based in Atherton had a team as early as 1915 and the women of the Preston Army Pay Corps had already played at Deepdale, the home of Preston North End Football Club in 1916, before Dick, Kerr Ladies. Other kinds of industrial welfare and generalist enthusiasm should therefore be acknowledged in this period. Lyons tearooms had several women's football teams too, for instance. Like other intended forms of «rational recreation», football could be used for the players' varied motivations and adapted to suit a variety of purposes. However, football seems to have been chosen by the players, rather than the management, as a preferred sport and leisure activity. It is now difficult to know whether players received payment in addition to expenses, but Lily Parr one of the most famous Dick, Kerr players was said to have received «broken time» payments of ten shillings a game in her career (Wiliams 2003: 25).

French female football teams were also founded by 1916: the Fédération des Sociétés Féminines Sportives de France (FSFSF) was established and organised a national championship for teams from Marseille, Reims, Paris and Toulouse. Alice Joséphine Marie Million, a young rower from Nantes in France, was to be an important figure for international women's sport (Drevon 2005: 5). Married and widowed relatively soon after, Alice Milliat worked as a translator and became President of the Femina women's sports club in 1915, three years after its formation by Pierre Payssé. In France, the exclusion of women from male sports federations had led to a rise in the number of sports clubs dedicated to their interests, such as En Avant. Académia, founded in 1915, supported a range of physical activities including natural movement dance inspired by Isadora Duncan; bicycling; football and rugby (or barette). A French national track and field athletics meeting in 1917 showcased some of the leading all-round sportswomen like javelin and shot-put enthusiast Violette Gourard Morris. «La Morris», as she became celebrated, was an imposing athlete who also boxed; swam; played football and drove cars professionally (Bouzanquet 2009: 24-5).

International games between women's teams coincided with more female participation. There were trials for an England team to play an Irish eleven in Belfast over Christmas 1917 in which the «Probables» took on the «Possibles» (Brennan 2007: 37). However, there remains a considerable amount of work to do to understand these games; some teams who called themselves England, Ireland or Scotland did so in order to sharpen local loyalties and should perhaps be considered work's teams. Alice Milliat became President of the Fédération des Sociétés Féminines Sportives de France (FSFSF) in 1919, and thereby inaugurated a national coalition of female sports clubs. Milliat first visited Preston in 1920 as a non-playing administrator with the Paris-based Fémina women's football team and was much impressed by the local hospitality and public support for the Dick, Kerr Ladies in Preston. In her subsequent career as an administrator and activist, she devoted considerable energy to promoting women's sports. With the expansion of the programme of the Olympic Games now overseen by the international federations of sport, rather than local organizing committees, Milliat targeted athletics as fundamental to the inclusion of more women in a greater range of disciplines. Team games nevertheless featured strongly in her vision for more democratic sport. Visits between Fémina and English teams, including Dick, Kerr's continued until well after World War Two.

Practical feminism of working-class women, combined with the political activism of the middle classes and civic boosterism. The games raised money for charities and their local communities respected women players. The inter-war period saw more European women eligible for the vote and a rise in the global processes related to sports, leisure and the entertainment industries more generally. Milliat led international versions of Women's Olympics from 1921, with the main events athletics, football and basketball matches drawing large crowds of up to 20,000 spectators, for instance. However, in response to crowds of up to 53,000 at Everton in 1920 and the supposed misuse of money raised for charity, the English governing body banned women's football from grounds of Association and League clubs on 5 December 1921. This was to have an effect on the continental mainland, especially about the «unsuitability» of football for women. When, in 1919, the Fédération Française de Football (FFF) was founded it refused to accept ladies' teams as members but did not institute a ban. European associations therefore had a rather haphazard approach to formal or informal prohibition (Williams 2007: 24).

The role of male players in helping women's teams also requires more analysis. For example, a club comprised of Fémina and other French players competed against the English team, Bridgett's United of Stoke, in Barcelona in 1923. The Stoke team was coached and escorted on the tour by Sunderland and England player Arthur Bridgett. Academic and family historians are finding out more about women's teams in this period all the time and the geographical spread likely to be more widespread than we so far understand (Munting 2007). Nevertheless, as an undesirable activity in the eyes of some leading European governing bodies, and with no Olympic presence so far as the IOC was concerned, one of the world's most popular sports was to have no official female international existence until 1970. This has profoundly shaped the image of football and female participation to this day, with resentment as to women's intrusion remaining a part of wider popular culture. So far as migration and professionalism however, there is emerging evidence of women travelling between Scotland, Ireland and the north of England to compete against one another and a growing number of teams in mainland European countries including France, Belgium and Spain. By 1923 Dick, Kerr's had travelled to the United States to play against male professional soccer teams but this was a short-lived experiment. There are fluxes between countries and flows of technical information from this period that require further academic attention.

In 1919 Austrian *Weekly Allgemeine Sport-Zeitung*, based in Vienna, reported matches; in 1920 a Frankfurt women's football team turned to rowing after public ridicule and by 1925 there were debates in *Sport und Sonne* about the essentially masculine nature of football, as one article headline indicated, «Das Fussbalspiel ist Männerspiel» (Hoffmann and Nendza 2006: 14). Thereafter, the German Football Association (Deutscher Fußball-Bund or DFB) regularly discouraged women from playing and banned men's teams from forming related women's squads. Notions of the body and permissiveness were, nevertheless, changing as the elegant «sport girl» exemplified by the willowy tennis player in whites and the «new woman» of boxing and athletics in the Weimar Republic graced the covers of *Sport und Sonne* in the 1930s (Jensen 2011: 25). In contrast, pioneers of women's football, like nineteen-year-old Lotte Specht, were making the Frankfurt weekly press looking very much like they had just played a hard match. Around 40 women played for DFC Frankfurt in 1930 while 850,000 female participants took part in the nationalistic gymnastics Turnen movement, so while numerically we would need to contextualise this activity, there is some emerging evidence of a history of female football as a European-wide activity (Nendza and Hoffmann 2006: 24).

Nevertheless, representatives of the female game were not party to the expansion of FIFA at a crucial period in the development of world football. By 1924 all the continental European countries had joined FIFA (though the English FA was to leave on more than one occasion until after World War Two). By 1928, football became more global, when the Southern hemisphere appeared on the cover of the FIFA handbook for the first time. In an effort to establish FIFA's independence from the International Olympic Committee and because of the success of the football tournament at the 1924 and 1928 Games (both won by Uruguay) the first World Cup was held in that country in 1930. However in terms of the history of international football the 1930 tournament has been argued to be localised rather than a world event, with Belgium, France, Romania and Yugoslavia the only four European countries present (Taylor 2006: 7-30). Uruguay won and the competition produced impressive financial returns. The World Cup hosted by Italy four years later took on a political dimension, due to Mussolini's presence, and the home team won in an intensely nationalistic atmosphere. The remaining inter-war competition took place in France in 1938 (won again by Italy). Lack of South American participation and European turmoil meant that the title of a World Cup was somewhat presumptuous and it was to be the last tournament for twelve years. At its resumption in Brazil in 1950, World Cup competition was thereafter to be an important means of stimulating football's world-wide development and commercial profile (Glanville 1980).

Establishing a European football confederation after World War Two was in part stimulated by anglo-continental antagonism, made worse by the insularity of the English Football Association and the Football League. This began to change slowly under the leadership of Stanley Rous. Wolverhampton Wanderers, one of the more successful Football League sides of the 1950s, was a pioneer of European competition, with friendly wins over FC Spartak Moscow in November 1954, amongst others. In a 1954 match against Kispest Honvéd FC of Hungary, Wolves came from behind to win 3-2, leading some British writers to claim them unofficial champions of Europe, if not club champions of the world (Taylor 2008: 265). *Hyperbole* was a British media trademark that could not go unchallenged: French sports journalist, Gabriel Hanot, writing for *L'Equipe* was not alone in finding this to be an arrogant claim. Competition on the continental mainland had included the central European Mitropa Cup (held since 1927) and the Latin Cup between teams from France, Italy, Portugal and Spain (held since 1949). Hanot, together with Jacques Ferran, designed a challenge tournament to be played on Wednesdays under floodlights and invited clubs on the basis of their attractiveness to supporters (Goldblatt 2007: 399). The newly-established competition faced typical English narrow-mindedness: for the inaugural European Champion Clubs' Cup in 1955-6 Scottish team Hibernian took part. English champions Chelsea wanted to, but did not, due to pressure from the national association and the Football League.

English attitudes to European football were changing though. The first game of the European Cup in September 1955 (which had the rather cumbersome title of the European Champion Clubs' Cup) showcased Sporting Lisbon against Partizan Belgrade and new standards of excellence. A young Bobby Charlton, who had broken into the Manchester United first team in the 1956-7 season, declared in an autobiography that he was «Under the Spell of Europe» at this time (2007: 109). In particular, Charlton was fascinated by the play of Alfred Di Stefano and thought him the complete player when United played Real Madrid in the semi-final of the competition. Real Madrid won five European trophies in a row between 1955-1960, just as British people began to own their first television sets.

Radio commentary had been a staple of the football fan since the early 1920s; now new kinds of European sporting glamour were shown on screens mid-week (Gundle 2008: 231). Paris, Rome and the Riviera were being referenced in other media industries, such as fashion and films, and as more people came to own their first colour television set, cosmopolitan football could also be broadcast to families in their own homes. Nor was this just an insight into Europe. Real Madrid's forwards included Argentina's Di Stefano, Hungary's Ferenc Puskas, France's Raymond Kopa and Gento. Defender José Santamaria of Uruguay also exemplified Madrid's international squad of players who were to monopolize the newly-inaugurated European Cup, in their all-white kit and light-weight boots.

Charlton's career was to become synonymous with European football as he and manager Matt Busby, survived the Munich Air Disaster of 6 February 1958. Returning from a European Cup match against Red Star Belgrade in Yugoslavia, the Manchester United team plane had stopped at Munich's Riem Airport to refuel and failed to take off in heavy snow. Eight of the team, commemorated from then on as Busby's Babes, were among the twenty-one dead. With Charlton at the centre of rebuilding the team, European Cup victory was not to come until 1968, two years after he had won a World Cup with England. Charlton released a series of four books for young readers on the subject of European football from 1969, focusing on key players. The multi-authored articles conveyed his enthusiasm for European competition as a key ambition for each season. Charlton therefore set an important lead: increasingly British players lower down the divisions aspired to compete in Europe (Taylor 2008: 205-8).

Commercial elements also saw the foundation of what was to become the UEFA Cup, as the Inter-Cities Fairs Cup, from April 1955 with ten teams. The original tournament lasted three years, with matches timed to coincide with trade fairs, before 1971/2, becoming known as the UEFA Cup. The change of name no longer associated the competition with trade fairs and has expanded from 1999/00 as domestic cup winners also qualified, after the UEFA Cup Winners' Cup was disbanded. Since 2009/10 the tournament has been known as the UEFA Europa League, with the group stage expanded to forty-eight clubs playing six matches on a home-and-away format. Of course, such commercial ventures were helped by the increase in air travel and improved transport links, with the attendant rise of personal motor ownership (scooters, motorbikes and cars) and collective journeys by land, sea and air. As a period of relative prosperity in Europe from the mid 1950s into the 1960s, with new forms of leisure and pleasure, football was one aspect of sports tourism to benefit from a wider fashionable cosmopolitanism. Paid holidays from work and rising incomes meant that travelling abroad became available for more people, though this should not be overstated. New and cheaper means of travel combined with increased communications accelerated and arguably democratized this trend in the later decades of the twentieth century and up to the present. Yet we know little about women in the Europeanisation of football; either as female fans; sporting tourists, players or coaches from the mid 1950s until the present day.

If these are recognized forces in the rise of the game, its cultural transfer and industrialisation, it is a less well-known aspect of football's history that twin forces obliged FIFA and UEFA to take control of women's participation between 1969 and 1971. The increasing numbers of female players combined with an attendant commercial interest in women's football. Nor was this particularly new, or down to some increased sense of permissiveness in European society by the late 1960s. Women had demonstrated awareness of European football providing new levels of competition during the first world war and tours like those undertaken by Dick, Kerr's continued until well after 1945. However, this became more widespread from 1955 onwards. Ingrid Heike and Ildiko Vaszil, for example, founded a club in spite of a West German ruling that women were not recognised by the DFB that year (Hoffmann and Nendza 2006: 32). The club joined a network, centred on Duisburg, to form a West German Women's Football Association with backing from Essen businessman Willi Ruppert. With Ruppert as the Chair of the self-titled German Ladies Football Association, six clubs in the Ruhr area played on communal pitches in front of around 5,000 spectators. An international game against the Netherlands took place in September 1956 at the Mathias-Stinnes-Stadion in Essen, with the usual national anthems and other conventions. Recorded for the weekly newsreel, Die Wochenschau and mediated across cinemas, Germany won in front of 18,000 fans including 1,000 Dutch spectators who saw their team lose 2-1. A second international in Munich in front of 17,000 spectators, saw media pronouncements that women's football had become fashionable, though tensions between the local council and the DFB over expenses and profits continued to make female play contentious.

A club competition, titled the European championship, was hosted under the auspices of an International Ladies' Football Association in 1957

(Eisenberg et al. 2004: 187). Teams from England, Austria, Luxembourg, the Netherlands and West Germany took part. Manchester Corinthians won the tournament, led by their 33 year-old captain, Doris Ashley and accompanied by professional football player Bert Trautmann, who acted as interpreter (ITN 1957). The Corinthians team had formed in 1949 and had already played against British and French opponents (Williams 2003: 54). Bert Trautmann was famously signed in 1949 by Manchester City for nothing and experienced anti-German feeling at the club early on, having chosen to remain in England after being released as a Prisoner of War. He then reached national acclaim by becoming the first goalkeeper, and foreigner, to be awarded the Football Writer's Association Footballer of the Year (for 1956), having helped Manchester City to win the FA Cup Final 3-1 against Birmingham. He received much public sympathy in Britain when his five-year old son was killed in a road traffic accident some months after the Cup Final. Manchester Corinthians were amateurs, whom Trautmann had first presented with the Festival of Britain trophy in 1951: one of many unofficial «national» tournaments for women's teams from the United Kingdom at the time. Doris Ashley's father was an enthusiastic local referee who had encouraged his daughter's interest in football and helped to coach the team.

The Corinthians' victory, supported by their famous interpreter, was a significant moment in the continuing Europeanisation of women's football. While Austria's Matthias Sindelar had supported Austrian women's teams in Vienna in 1935, and England's Tom Finney had been a schoolmate of Dick, Kerr's player Joan Whalley, the 1957 tournament was a consciously European competition. Large crowds were recorded on the newsreels and suggested a latent market for women's football, even at this time (Williams 2003: 25). We do not know the extent to which female players' interest was stimulated by the 1954 West German World Cup victory in Switzerland, 3-2 over the favourites Hungary: the Miracle of Bern. Nor has anyone assessed the effect of UEFA's European Cup on female football participation. We do know, however, that the Manchester Corinthians toured Portugal in 1957-8; Madeira in 1958; South America and Ireland in 1960; Italy in 1961; Morocco and North Africa in 1966. Many of these exhibition and charity matches were organised by the International Red Cross and were played on major grounds in front of large crowds (Lopez 1997: 21-2).

This is, of course, just one team. With further research at the individual and club-level, more evidence of this emerging transnational community of women players will no doubt emerge. Without going into further details, the point is that there were financial and popular interests involved in the post-war women's game well before it was accepted by the national and international governing bodies of football. Women's football teams were around in Austria, Czechoslovakia; Denmark; England; Finland; France; Luxembourg, the Netherlands; Norway; Scotland; Sweden, the USSR and West Germany in the 1950s and 1960s. Increasing access to contemporary media sources will help researchers to uncover more of these activities. Slavia Praha and CKD Slany played in a regular Czech tournament of the 1960s, including a «Gingerbread Heart Final» in 1969 for instance (Williams 2007: 48). By 1963 Germany's women had played a reported seventy «unofficial» international games when they marked the occasion with a 4-0 defeat over Holland, with Maron, a former player with Borussia Dortmund, as their manager. A conscious policy of the DFB, mirrored in England, of encouraging women teachers to instruct football-drills in schools, seems to have empowered some degree of female recognition, even if the distinction between a teacher's certificate and a coaching badge was to remain an important one. The history of Europe's female coaches and managers is another monograph waiting to be completed.

According to my interviews with players like Sue Lopez for this research, Italian physical education lecturer Mira Bellei was instrumental to the formation of the Roma women's team in 1967. Roma was to become an important club for migrating players, especially the British, who played alongside Italian internationals, such as the striker Stefania Medri and centre-back Lucia Gridelli. By 17 May 1968 nine Italian women's football teams had announced formation of the Federazione Italiana Calcio Femminile (FICF) in Viareggio (Ambrosiana, Cagliari, Fiorentina, Genova, Lazio, Napoli, Milano, Piacenza and Roma) with Real Torino joining a year later (*The Times*, 18 May 1968: 8). In November 1969 another attempt was made to co-ordinate activities on the continent through the establishment of a Fédération Internationale Européenne de Football Féminin (FIEFF), with the sponsorship of the aperitif drink company Martini and Rossi. Turin hosted a tournament where teams representing Italy, Denmark, England and France were provided with kit, equipment, all-expenses paid travel and accommodation. This was another milestone in a European-wide awareness of the women's game. The Turin tournament, for example, drew in English players like Sue Lopez; Sue Buckett; Jill Long; Barbara Birkett; Dorothy «Dot» Cassell and Joan Clements, some of whom returned to Italy to join one of the teams there. Denmark's Birgit Nilsen and Czech national Maria Scevikova also played in Italy.

A second Italian professional women's league, the Federazione Femminile Italiana Gioco Calcio (FFIGC), was established in Rome in 1970 with fourteen teams. The resulting women's world championship there in 1970 and another in Mexico in 1971 meant that businessmen independent of the governing bodies had begun to explore the commercial potential of female football at the elite level. This time concern was shown by both FIFA and UEFA. Circular letter 142 of 1970 asked FIFA member nations to indicate if women's football existed in their countries and instructed them to take control of all forms that they found (FIFA 1973: 1). At the 1971 Extraordinary UEFA Congress in Monte Carlo the Vice President, Sandor Barcs, gave a speech on women's football. Barcs reported that women already played in twenty-two European countries, but only eight national associations controlled female football (FIFA 1974a: 2). The French and West German national associations were the first to reverse their neglect of the women's game and the English FA followed by overturning its ban in 1971. The year was a defining moment in European football, as UEFA agreed that all its national associations should take control of women's participation (FIFA 1974b: 1). Incorporation was followed by a decade in which official recognition was often grudging.

Although Europe and North America were important, an Asian Ladies Football Association (ALFA) had been formed in Hong Kong in 1968 and had tried to affiliate to FIFA as a confederation in its own right (FIFA 1980: 2). There was therefore international pressure and sufficient knowledge about the wider transnational community of women's teams to exert pressure on FIFA, as well as the confederations. The emergence of leadership and commercial interest, plus the growth in female participants, created a degree of community cohesion in women's football. This required acknowledgement. One of my two main critiques of globalisation theories as grand narratives about sport is that they are rarely sensitive to the role of women in the diffusion of sport in the nineteenth and early twentieth century. The second is that such work often ignores voluntary networks of community, evident in formal and informal ties of affiliation and goodwill. Most sport worldwide, especially at the youth level, is dependent on armies of volunteers who mentor and encourage young people. Very few

athletes are privileged enough to earn a living solely from sport. However, much more academic work has concerned elite, adult male football
at the end of the twentieth century and into the twenty-first. This ignores
the mass of players who have pursued sport in its history, often subsidis-
ing their own playing careers, supported by the altruism of others, from
childhood onwards. Given that the history of organised modern football
is largely about how the games of children became the work of adults and
were then professionalised at ever younger ages, this seems to be a general
academic oversight in need of redress.

The women's game became gradually incorporated within UEFA and
FIFA after 1971 but without being commercialised. Three separate meetings discussed the issue in 1971 and the confederation founded a Committee for Women's Football to hold regular meetings and to organise
a European Championship (UEFA 1973: 2). The first memorandum on
women's football was approved at UEFA's 1972 Vienna Congress. In the
earliest meetings to discuss women's football, female speakers were conspicuous by their absence, though Pat Gregory attended as an observer. In
1973 UEFA officials decided: «To wait for about two years before introducing a women's competition» (UEFA 1973: 4). It would actually take
another nine years. Meanwhile, Mr Boll, from Switzerland, reported that
his daughter had been playing professionally in Italy since 1971 where
matches drew ten to fifteen thousand spectators, especially in Viareggio and La Spezia. Mr Boll continued that some companies were paying
400,000 Swiss Francs a year in sponsorship and publicity to be associated
with the league. The meeting agreed in response to boycott FIEFF activities and the world championship in Mexico 1971. In addition, members
circulated a memorandum from UEFA to the Federazione Italiana Giuoco
Calcio (FIGC), the Italian Football Federation to the effect that no female
team was to play against a male side and no woman player was allowed to
sign for a male club.

Dr Kersten Rosén became the first woman speaker when she addressed
the UEFA committee on women's football in Zurich on 21 March 1973
(FIFA 1981: 2). A conference on women's football followed the next day.
Nine member associations attended and examined the results of a survey
of member associations. After the conference, the committee met again
but no decisions regarding competition or development were taken (UEFA
1980: 2). A survey followed in 1974 but produced a limited response. After a period of inactivity, UEFA dissolved the Women's Football Commit-

tee in 1978. At this time, Italy had three female associations: two merged, one disbanded and the reconfigured group invited both official and unofficial European women's football associations to a meeting in the country, scheduled for April 1980. UEFA responded to this by hosting its own second conference on women's football at the Hotel Atlantic, Lisbon. It involved twenty-nine delegates from eighteen member associations of the thirty-four affiliated to UEFA in that year (FIFA 1984: 3). The eighteen national associations present were Austria; Belgium; Czechoslovakia; Denmark; England; Finland; France; FR Germany; GD Germany; Republic of Ireland; Italy; the Netherlands; Norway; Portugal; Scotland; Sweden; Switzerland and Wales. Four women attended: England's Pat Gregory; Germany's Hannelore Ratzeburg; Belgium's Frau Vandelaanoote and Norway's Ellen Wille (UEFA 1980: 2). Summary documents showed participation levels in the following countries: Denmark 26,000 female players; England 4,000; Finland 3,000; France 6,000; West Germany 111,000; Holland 11,000; Sweden 9,400 and Belgium (plus the remaining countries) with 2,500 or fewer competitors. A five-person committee for European competition was again reinstated and this was ratified at the June 1980 UEFA Congress. The Committee returned to the issue of a competition, anticipating that a maximum of twelve national teams would be able to field squads (club-level tournaments being judged as unfeasible). When this was announced, the number of applicants exceeded expectations and sixteen national football associations entered women's teams (UEFA 1982: 1).

In the period between 1971 and 1981, the women's game was perceived as amateur so sponsorship was turned down and lost at national and international level. The DFB, for example, allowed its sixteen regions to organise championships at that level, before seeing a private initiative launch a national championship in 1972-3. The DFB then took this over without sponsors the following season and familiar names like TuS Worrstadt; Bonner SC; Bayern Munich; SSG Bergisch Gladbach and SC Bad Neuenahr; KBC Duisburg; FSV Frankfurt and TEV Siegen won the German championship between 1974-1996 (UEFA 1984: 2). The unofficial Asian-based international tournaments continued to be important for European teams, and particularly for domestic recognition. It was only after Bergisch Gladbach had won the tournament in Taiwan in 1981 that the DFB decided to create a West German women's national squad for 1982. There were 3,000 female football clubs at this time from which the players could be selected.

An opportunity to stage a Women's World Championship in England was also declined in 1972/3 because a cutlery company, Viners, wanted to sponsor the event to the tune of £150,000 (Lopez 1997: 62-3). Given that the World Cup in England in 1966 had seen previously unprecedented forms of commercialisation of goods and services (with the first mascot, World Cup Willie, the first official song and numerous other items of merchandise) the decision to turn down Viners' offer of sponsorship looked to be out of step with the industry as a whole. But it was to be 1991 and the M&M's Women's World Championship in PR China, before FIFA was to get over its squeamishness about accepting sponsorship from a multinational, in this case, a confectionary brand.

The narrative about women's football began to change with more technical consideration of the standard of play after the inauguration of UEFA competitions in 1982. There was less concern about whether women should be allowed to play than how well biology would allow them to perform (FIFA 1984: 2). The sixteen-team 1982 UEFA-sponsored competition therefore indicated significant engagement by the confederation with female elite players. The Competition for National Women's Representative Teams, as it was titled, was nevertheless highly regionalised and held over two-years in the following groupings:
- Group 1: Sweden, Iceland, Finland, Norway.
- Group 2: England, Northern Ireland, Republic of Ireland, Scotland.
- Group 3: Italy, France, Portugal, Spain.
- Group 4: Belgium, Switzerland, Denmark, FR Germany.
The inaugural trophy was won by Sweden in one of the more competitive groups (UEFA 1982: 3).

A meeting to review the experiment left UEFA ambivalent, having devoted a yearly contribution of 25,000 Swiss Francs to the first competition (UEFA 1984: 2). Inauspicious as this may have seemed, women's football became more trans-European and international because the relative strengths of the continent's national teams were showcased in a formally-endorsed competition. This stimulated increased domestic interest in women's football in some countries, at the same time as intensifying international rivalries (FIFA 1985: 2). More sustained and specialised preparation for such competitions consequently became more widespread. At a meeting in Geneva, chaired by Carl Nielsen, and attended by Pat Gregory and Hannelore Ratzeburg along with UEFA President, Jacques Georges, and General Secretary, Hans Bangerter, a small budget was approved for

the second European tournament. This caused the groups to be reconfigured in 1984 to limit the need for travel (UEFA 1984: 4-6):
- Group 1: FR Germany, Denmark, Finland, Norway.
- Group 2: England, Northern Ireland, Republic of Ireland, Scotland.
- Group 3: Belgium, France, The Netherlands, Sweden.
- Group 4: Italy, Switzerland, Spain, Hungary.

The new tournament was therefore shaped by old ways of thinking. Proposals included that it be played over three years to avoid a clash with the finals of the FIFA (men's) World Cup or the UEFA European Championships and the next edition did not take place until 1987. In the Final, Norway beat Sweden in Oslo, supported by 8,500 spectators, by two goals to one. Another idea for a FIFA backed female invitational tournament, possibly to be staged in Japan in 1987, was felt by UEFA officials to be premature (FIFA 1986a: 2). The same meeting decided that it was not the task of UEFA to carry out experiments in girls' or women's football, rather this was the role of FIFA and national associations. At the Final of the third competition under UEFA jurisdiction, held in Osnabruck in July 1989, Germany beat Norway by four goals to one. The 1989/91 tournament was retitled the First European Championship for Women's Football. With eighteen participants, for the first time, more than half of the UEFA member associations took part.

The European competitions provided a vital precursor for the Women's World Cups, not least in slowly persuading football's bureaucracies of the playing-standard of women's football relative to the male game (FIFA 1988: 6). This can be seen by the dominance of European berths in Women's World Cup Finals, which have been as many as five of a twelve-team tournament (FIFA 1991: 3). The widening of the number of teams in the Canadian Women's World Cup Finals in 2015 to twenty-four, marks an expansion of opportunities for non-European countries therefore. It also demonstrates a combined world-wide increase in female participation and ever-growing institutional support for women's competitions. FIFA announced that at its meeting on 17 December 2002 the FIFA Executive Committee had decided that at least 4% of annual payments received by national associations should be allocated to women's football (2002: 4). While this has now increased incrementally again by 2011 to 10%, there is much that could be done financially in hard cash and soft diplomacy to enhance women's place in the industry as a whole.

In concluding this introduction then, before looking at the relation-ship between sources and methods in the next chapter, we can say that, from a point of view of European football's officialdom, women's soccer was a relative latecomer to sporting competition. It is debatable at what point women's football and nationalism became synonymous but the very patriotic showing of Women's World Cup 1999 in Los Angeles (just five years after the men's World Cup in the United States in 1994) provides an important starting point for this analysis. The event in Sweden in 1995 did not really catch the public imagination because it was scheduled in conjunction with an athletics event. So Germany 2011 was an opportunity to sell a World Cup only five years after a men's event and to mark sev-eral European «firsts» in the women's game. Perhaps this pattern will see Women's World Cup 2019 go to Brazil to do the same in South America.

The early period of enthusiasm for European football from the mid-1950s, which appeared to centre on male forms of the game, was also important for women's football. By the 1970s football's image was tar-nished by the exposure of bribery scandals and hooliganism which one commentator has called «Eurosclerosis» (King 2003: 49-69). This wider context helps us to understand that female players were part of an emerg-ing sense of European competition during the 1950s and 1960s. We can also see that football's governing bodies integrated the women's game in part to appear more inclusive in response to a wider «legitimacy-crisis» in the 1970s and 1980s. Accepting women players appeared to make the industry look more progressive but power and prestige have been slow to follow. In 2012 Lydia Nsekera, the President of the Burundi Football Association and a member of the Committee for Women's Football and the FIFA Women's World Cup and of the Organising Committee for the Olympic Football Tournaments, became the first woman co-opted member of the FIFA Executive Committee. In the framework of the FIFA reform process, it was agreed that the twenty-fifth member of the FIFA Executive Committee would become an elected representative. Four confederations proposed a candidate for the election in May 2013: Moya Dodd, Lydia Nsekera, Sonia Bien-Aime and Paula Kearns. Europe and South America therefore became the two confederations not to have nominated a candi-date for the role. Acceptance for women players and administrators have re-positioned the governing bodies as less conservative than they had been until that point. Change was, and is still, a very slow process (Williams 2003: 143-4).

Arguably it was not until the success of Women's World Cup 1999 in the United States (where thirty four UEFA member associations expressed a wish to participate in the tournament) that the commercial prospects for women's football became a priority for the sport's governing bodies (UEFA 2001a and 2001b). The first-ever European competition for women's football, the «Women's Euro» beginning in 1982 nevertheless helped this procedure. The inaugural tournament was won by a Pia Sundhage penalty for Sweden to beat England for the title. However, Sundhage's international career was to last twenty-one years between 1975 and 1996. As the sixth ranked player in the FIFA Woman Player of the Century poll, what changes did she, and other players like her, experience before and after official European competition became established? What can individual migration patterns to earn a living from the game tell us about the status of women's football then and now? How have women become part of the technocracy of the sport since then; as players, coaches; media commentators and administrative leaders?

Of course, the nature of football as an industry changed in the late 1980s and early 1990s, with male migrant counterparts now increasingly visible, especially in English, French, German, Italian and Spanish leagues. Poli et al. concluded that 93.3% of male Arsenal players and were expatriates in 2010 and the top ten teams in the Champions' League for that year had percentages of overseas players of roughly 70% and above (2010: 44). Fien Timisela, from the Netherlands, is an example of the generation following Pia Sundhage as a player-turned coach who can earn at least part of her living in the United States. Previously a Dutch National Team and futsal (indoor soccer) team player, and now working as the head coach of the KFC Koog aan de Zaan, Fien also works for part of the year at the Dutch Soccer Academy in the United States. In terms of her transportable skills and qualifications, Fien has the prestigious TC3 coaching degree from the KNVB. She began her coaching career by training young men at under fifteen years of age and she eventually coached the women's team in Castricum. With linguistic barriers that can be overcome by the primarily visual and physical nature of the game, we can begin to think of football skills as like other transportable technical abilities. There are currently three main semi-professional female football leagues established in Germany, the Netherlands and England (plus numerous national competitions, especially in Scandinavia, France and more western European countries). While a limited European market for women football players appears evident, there are more world-wide opportunities for women to earn a living from the sport than at any previous time in history (Zhenqi 1982: 2).

3. Conclusion

UEFA has been by far the most influential instigator of international com-petition for women's football of the six confederations. While this work draws upon the broader context, it essentially focuses on developments in the 1960s leading to the first Monte Carlo conference on women's football in 1971 and ending with the approaching Women's World Cup in Canada in 2015. This introductory section has looked at the growth of European competitions as a wider framework for the more specific migration pat-terns of professional and semi professional women moving into, and out of, Europe (Collins 2006: 353).

The subsequent chapters use both micro and macro examples to ex-amine the «push» and «pull» factors influencing individual women play-ers and the football labour markets open to them. Increasing numbers of women wanted to play professionally and they moved into and out of Europe from the early 1970s onwards. Asia, Canada and the United States have been important to the world-wide development of female player op-portunities (Chye Hin 1981: 3, Close et al 2006: 25). The work looks at the meso level of development from the mid 1980s in order to assess the improved European-wide opportunities for women shortly after changes in world-football. As well as specific changes in the women's game, these more favourable conditions followed the Hillsborough disaster in 1989; the *Taylor Report* requirement of all-seater stadia in England and the ne-gotiations for what would be the first Premier League season in August 1992. Often perceived as part of the feminization and embourgeoisement of football, these recent changes have to be seen against a longer history of female involvement since at least the 1880s (Harris 2001 and 2005).

The Premiership began to organize its own broadcast and sponsorship agreements at a time when many clubs had also floated on the Stock Mar-ket to become PLCs and brands in their own right. The sums of money in-volved prompted clubs to take on community-based projects and women's football generally benefitted from this aspect of Corporate Social Responsibility. Most high-profile men's clubs will have an affiliated women's team, but the degree of support and genuine partnership varies as the contrasting fortunes of Arsenal and Manchester United's women's teams show. There are also important independent women's clubs that do not fit this wider trend to consider. Finally, in looking at a nascent professional market with specially-established leagues, competitions and tournaments the macro-level section seeks to ask, what has been Europe's role in the global game for women?

Football's universal qualities have made it a focal point for international interaction and cross-cultural exchange. Playing the game does not require the use of a specific national language, and the rules for both the men's and women's game have long been standardised across the globe. As such, the international football market could be considered one of the best examples of a genuinely transnational and multicultural employment sector. We need to do more work on the forms of migration and commercialism of the female game as part of the political economy of football. It is a so far hidden aspect of the social, cultural and historic dimensions of the industry. The next chapter on methods and sources has three overlapping themes therefore. Firstly, global claims for football have tended to underplay the individual and the local experience. Secondly, the chapter argues the need to gender the research questions of the study of sport, football in particular. Thirdly, for the most part, though not entirely, football consists of individuals, local to a geographical place or space.

These individuals and groups have clustered together in informal and formal networks who may, or may not, interact with the powerful bureaucracies who oversee the game at national, continental and world levels. In order to begin to look at this, we have to ask the players themselves where football fits into their wider life experience. It is to be hoped that more quantitative analyses will follow this qualitative study. Painstaking as the qualitative and quantitative work is, the micro level of women's experience as football's talented and knowledgeable migrants is not yet widely-discussed. The emergent forms of professionalism pioneered by individual women in the later decades of the twentieth century tell us much about how football has been experienced and performed in the lives of those who would like to turn an amusing game into serious, but rewarding, work.

Sources and Methods

*Our perspective on the past alters. Looking back, immediately in front of
us is dead ground. We don't see it, and because we don't see it this means
that there is no period so remote as the recent past. And one of the historian's jobs is to anticipate what our perspective of that period will be
(Bennett 2004: 74).*

1.   The academic literature on women's football, professional leagues and migration

Football's migrants include those who have settled for a short time, emi-
grated for longer periods and settled for life. First of all then, it is important to distinguish how movement is fundamentally related to migration,
but also has its own distinct patterns of space and time. World-wide diffusion had been a feature of modern football since the nineteenth century
(Tischler 1981, Walvin 1994). Soccer spread to the populations of indus-
trialized Europe; countries in South America, Africa, Asia, Oceania and
onwards. However, the international governance of the game remained
Euro-centric in spite of autonomous football cultures developing in South
America (Lanfranchi 1994). Football did not become truly global until
after the Second World War when FIFA witnessed an unprecedented increase in membership. As the introductory comments have shown, affiliates included new post-colonial sovereign states. FIFA's World Cup,
like the Olympic Games, provided a highly mediated showcase in which
newly independent nation states could compete.

   The creation of UEFA was partly a response to the perceived need for
Europe to re-assert its place in the emerging football world order. Only in
1970 were Asia and Africa each allocated a place in the men's World Cup
finals for the first time (Glanville 1980: 186). It was not until 1998 that an
expanded tournament admitted five teams from Africa and four from Asia
among the thirty-two finalists. However claims for football's global ten-
dencies often argue that the sport has helped to homogenise world culture,
largely as a product of the expansion of capitalist mercantile aspirations,

driven by greater connectivity in media and communications technology (Boyle and Haynes 2004: 5). Giulianotti and Robertson go further to argue that the rapid commercial transformation of the industry as a whole means that it is possible to talk about the «footballization» of national and global economies (2009: 63).

As the differing attitudes to boys and girls on the same team (or more contentiously men and women) in what is called «mixed football» demonstrate, the sport can have radically different meanings in contrasting national contexts. Masculinity may be part of the historical development of the game and policed by convention in some countries, while in others, the association game is perceived as more feminine than other team games considered to be more violent or hyper-masculine. Football's standardized transnational codes have also been inflected by regional and local meanings. Academics now talk about the global in the local (branded products worn by players having a kick-around on a local park) and the local in the global (Leicester City Football Club merchandise on sale in Thai airport shops run by the owners King Power). This research therefore resists the overarching narrative that globalization seems to offer in favour of a more detailed analysis (Bairner 2001: 174). The sources for this research have been drawn from individuals; groups and communities as well as the archives of elites. Transnational fluxes in player migration and expertise, large as these may be, are still far from making football a global female experience.

Having cultivated a paying public for women's football for a brief period during and after World War One, talented female players became the object of national or regional pride. There were also economic advantages in the form of public receptions; civic recognition; broken time payments and prestige. Many played for the sheer fun. As an emerging spectacle, the 1921 ban on women's football set a reputation that remained for fifty years. It would be difficult to over-state how damaging this exclusion was. Barbara Keys has shown that the 1930s generally saw:

> The most significant internationalization [...] in the realm of elite, high-achievement sport. Here a truly transnational culture was established, one that attained an existence independent of the countries participating in it (2006: 10).

Sport became the leading form of physical culture in Europe during this period, displacing both gymnastics and worker's recreation. The interplay of national and international identities was an inherent aspect of this, in spite of challenging economic, political and social circumstances. Given the array of sporting enthusiasms more open to women and the variety of easily available leisure pursuits, female football participation remained under-developed world-wide. Nevertheless, for a significant minority, the enduring popularity of football provided a degree of autonomy and this persisted during the social and cultural change in Europe after World War Two. The main effect of the successes enjoyed by those active in charitable games of women's football was to enhance the morale of local people, in spite of Dick, Kerr's claims to be the world leading team. By the time of the victory of the Manchester Corinthians in Germany in 1957, football's regional pride and national rhetoric had well established female forms. However, it was only in the last three decades of the twentieth century that internationalism and professionalism became pressing issues for the governing bodies of the sport. Consequently, different kinds of network and interconnecting communities were significant in women's football. The informal pathways of movement could be more important than formal connections.

Not least, there was little or no infrastructure to encourage participation at various national associations until at least 1970; in most cases these systems developed ten or twenty years later (Abrahams 2005, Adderley 2006). In 1970 a FIFA-conducted survey to its one hundred and thirty nine constituent affiliated national associations produced ninety responses, only twelve of which replied in favour of endorsing the women's game (FIFA 1973: 2). While women's football had a longer history than FIFA's involvement, the world governing body consequently describe it as having «begun» over a hundred years after the sport was first codified and is therefore often perceived as in its «infancy» (FIFA 2002). While this periodization and language has been addressed in this work as an invented tradition of the sporting bureaucracies, it is also clear that the many alternative attempts to establish women's football were not sustained (Hobsbawm 1990, Hobsbawm and Ranger 1992). In theorizing this, I am by no means the first to have drawn on Benedict Anderson's term «imagined communities» to outline an «Imagined world of modern sport [...] based on a fraternity of elites, among both the athletes who garnered public adulation and the officials who wielded power behind the scenes» (1991: 14). Though Anderson is now somewhat dismissive and thinks the term a cliché because the phrase has been so widely adapted, there is some use, I think, in asking who are the wider «imagined community» of fans who might become the consumers and supporters of professional women's football in Europe? By the time of increased female involvement after 1945, world football had developed complex systems, business practices and a social cachet that made female involvement appear to be new and different (Glanville 1973). Rather than exclude female players altogether, the bureaucracies began to normalise a restrictive set a circumstances called «women's football».

As the introductory comments outlined, UEFA had discussed women's international and professional football extensively since the 1971 extraordinary Congress of Monte Carlo. Yet there is little written on subsequent developments leading to professionalism in the women's game. There has been a sustained popular and academic consideration of women's football since the first PhD on the subject by Ali Melling (1999). The Dick, Kerr's team has a popular history (Williamson 1991, Newsham 1998, Jacobs 2004, Brennan 2007). Sue Lopez's key text *Women on the Ball* has however been the most useful text for this study as it has both an international, comparative perspective and uses interviews from key individuals in the history of women's football (1997).

The history of male football migration includes contemporary texts (Gibson and Pickford 1906) in addition to academic studies (Fishwick 1989). These became more developed with work informed by the wider academic literature on the dynamic of migration and transfer (Bale and Maguire 1994, Lanfranchi and Taylor 2001). There are now several articles and chapters on female experiences of playing football (Caudwell 1999 and 2002, Highfield Oral History Group and the Sir Norman Chester Centre for Football 1993, Jinxia 2002, Mennesson and Clement 2003, Munting 2007, Myotin 1999, Nelson 1996, Scraton et al. 2005). The key publication for migration has been Sine Agergaard and Vera Bothelo *Female Football Migration: Motivational Factors for Early Migratory Processes* (2010). However, there are texts that look at country specific developments useful for looking at cultural transfer (Marschik 1998, Prudhomme-Poncet 2003, Markovits and Hellermann 2003).

Even when football is now played world-wide, local variations in the women's game mean that assumptions of football's global penetration, as a participation sport; as a cultural industry and as a social phenomenon require reconsideration. A number of articles address the economic and structural features of the markets in which professional sports teams operate (Rottenberg 1956, Neale 1964, Sloane 1971). Neale, in particular, debated the distinctive mix of cooperation and competition that characterizes sports markets and the «fourth estate benefit» of selling a sport by media coverage through radio, TV and newspaper sports writers. Stephen Hardy developed the role of entrepreneurs, major organizations and the wider sports marketplace (1986 and 1997). Dilwyn Porter has more recently explored the intersection of sport, politics and business history (2004). There has yet to be a comparatively detailed analysis of the economics of women's sports.

Nevertheless, the longer historical views help to critically evaluate the claims for football's globalisation supported by large financial figures at the extreme end of professionalism. At the turn of the millennium, annual football-related business was estimated at around 250 billion Euros, with the 2006/7 season in Europe valued at 13.6 billion Euros (Deloitte 2008: 5). In England alone, the twenty Premiership clubs' share of 2.3 billion Euros, was a two-hundred per cent increase on the previous decade and nine times higher than when the League began. It is easy to see why such large sums lead to big claims for political-economic explanations when, in 2004, 1.7% of the Spanish gross national product involving 66,000 jobs, for example, was estimated to be generated by football (Deloitte 2008: 5). For the historian of women's football, these figures are a reminder how rapidly the industry as a whole has changed, at the same time that male professionals in the majority of leagues and female players who are trying to innovate viable careers, experience nothing like the benefits available to the few stars in the big world franchises.

Each of these strands of literature has provided an element of the framework to approach a pan-European understanding of professional women's football. Taken together with the literature on football itself, they offer a reminder that the game of football has often been credited with meanings and influences beyond sport. Specifically, what has become called «women's football» tends to homogenise female experience as similar, and fundamentally different to that of men. When life-course, ethnicity, sexuality, religious belief, disability, affluence, education and family history are also taken into account this can be questioned. Issues of inclusion and exclusion are highlighted by the assumption that the quintessentially masculine game requires a modifying adjective.

2.   Labour markets and women's football

Women's participation in football grew unevenly and was challenged by the established elites. In consequence female professionalism grew piece-meal, often pioneered by individuals and small groups. Player and ad-ministrator interviews have been used to elucidate how some of the most important figures perceived their experiences. Archival evidence and elite administrator interviews provided data on the expansion of international tournaments, along with my own collection of women's football fanzines and memorabilia since the early 1980s. Finally, attendance at tournaments as a guest researcher (such as Women's World Cup in 1999 and 2003 in the USA); consultations with elite administrators and attendance at UEFA events; archival evidence and player interviews helped to contextualise the establishment of professional women's leagues beginning with the Women's United Soccer Association (WUSA) in 2000.

If the small percentage of female players in the overall participant pop-ulation is note-worthy, some of the big numbers around women's football also caution against a story of relentless expansion. The WUSA league began its first season in April 2001 with eight teams in the United States. Among these eight teams, a spread of twenty founding United States na-tional team players were drafted and became shareholders of the franchise. It was a co-operative model that signalled player empowerment and has not been reproduced elsewhere subsequently. It had considerable cross-over appeal: American talk show host David Letterman christened the women's national team «Babe City». Up to four international players were allowed on each squad as a «foreign draft» and attracted migrant groups of players from the stronger elite countries and individual talents from oth-ers. Though WUSA was primarily intended to provide professional em-ployment for United States national team players, the league also aimed to be a breakthrough for women's football world-wide. For a brief three seasons, it achieved that aim. In spite of backing from John Hendricks, founder of the Discovery channel, the league suspended operations on 15 September 2003 at the end of its third season, after making cumulative losses of around US$ 100 million. Originally forecast as requiring eight corporate sponsors to spend US$ 2.5 million each per year to remain vi-able, only Hyundai and Johnson and Johnson agreed to that commitment. WUSA's average attendance also slipped from 8,000 to 6,700 a game, a drop of 5% in live support. Some blamed player wages, others a failure to tie in investors for long-term partnerships and all agreed that the economic downturn after 11 September 2001 added to the league's demise.

WUSA was the most high profile professional league for women's football in history and it seemed to draw in playing personnel from all over the globe. Among the notable talents were PR China's Sun Wen, Pu Wei, Fan Yunjie, Zhang Ouying, Gao Hong, Zhao Lihong, and Bai Jie. This is not surprising as they had played against the US team in the 1999 WWC Finals in front of 93,000 fans at the Rosebowl stadium, losing only on penalties. Strikers like Kelly Smith of England and Germany's Birgit Prinz were increasingly important to the overall competitiveness of the games. Foreign strikers were seen as key to the excitement of the franchise in order to increase the number of goals scored and increase appeal to television audiences. Germany's other players included Conny Pohlers, Steffi Jones and Maren Meinert. They were joined by Norway's Hege Riise, Unni Lehn and Dagny Mellgren. Not all of the migrants were European: Brazil's Sissi, Katia and Pretinha also obtained employment. Canada's Charmaine Hooper, Sharolta Nonen and Christine Latham played at least one season. In addition, the league employed Maribel Dominguez of Mexico. Homare Sawa of Japan, Julie Fleeting of Scotland, Cheryl Salisbury of Australia and Marinette Pichon of France. The failure of the league was read in some quarters as a synechdoche for the lack of viability of women's football, and female sports spectacle, globally. However, there were benefits such as an improvement in the overall standard of elite play as a result of regular competition, just as there were critics. Rather than grand narratives and generalisations, this work seeks to nuance aspects of female professionalism in order to assess the individual gains against the general challenges.

The ethnographic techniques such as participant observation and player interviews sought to explore the impetus for professionalism as part of an individual woman's overall career in football. The focus on Europe was in part because UEFA funded the research and also because of challenges of time and space. The players selected have all had international careers and future research projects could include those who were not part of an elite. It would also be interesting to know how many women went into other sports in order to better support themselves. However, given that we know individuals like England's Sue Lopez and Scotland's Rose Reilly had to choose a professional club or an amateur international career in the early 1970s, we can see evidence of transnational markets for good women players. The micro evidence overlaps with the meso and the macro phases of professionalism. For example, the format of the second Women's World Cup of 1995 in Sweden, was combined with an athletics event because of perceptions of an under-developed spectator base for women's football. This was not a success. Social change, new technologies and adapted formats have proliferated the number of copyrighted tournaments endorsed by the world governing body include the following: the FIFA Beach Soccer World Cup; FIFA Interactive World Cup; Blue Stars/FIFA Youth Cup; FIFA Club World Cup; FIFA Futsal World Cup; FIFA U-20 Women's World Cup and the Youth Olympic Games competition held in Singapore in 2010 where Chile and Bolivia were respective winners in the girls' and boy's competitions. These are not the entire trophy product range for FIFA but it is possible to see that logistical and leadership aspects of tournaments provide new kinds of transnational work for more people in football. As such, female graduates of sports business, law and administration courses provide another cohort for future researchers, as many may have decided to make a career out of sport after first becoming players.

Women's football joined the international competitive stage in 1982 if we use the UEFA competitions as a European indicator, or in 1991, if we use the World Cup competitions as a marker. The professional aspects of association football can still lag behind more popular sports and leisure activities for women world-wide. This is partly a problem of sport generally and those involving risk, endurance or contact generally. A woman's marathon was not included in Olympic competition until 1984, for instance, and many of the female pioneers like Joan Benoit and Grete Waitz had to run other distances in official competitions until then. However, running for fitness and as a participation sport has seen an exponential rise in female commercialisation since the mid-1980s. Avon, the cosmetics company, took on distance race sponsorship well before women became integrated with the London Marathon in 1980 for example. The migration of African women to compete in valuable races across the world, in order to become millionaires through their performance and endorsements is an interesting aspect of this different labour-market. It is quite likely that there are more women in Africa who have been made wealthy through running as professionals than those who have done so through football, but more research remains to confirm this hypothesis. Individual sports involving contact, like boxing, continue to attract some women away from football's relatively under-developed infrastructure. Although it was included as an Olympic event only in 2012, gold medal winner, Ireland's Katie Taylor, may well earn more money from endorsements related to her boxing activity than her football career. Before winning gold, Taylor had already as appeared in a Lucozade commercial sparring, to the tune «Simply Unstoppable» with Tinnie Tempah and Blink 182 drummer Travis Barker.

Given the broadly amateur nature of women's football in Europe to this day, the effects of Title IX legislation in the United States of America, made college-based soccer an increasingly popular specialism in a decade when the first female Olympic competition was to be held in Atlanta in 1996 and the Los Angeles Women's World Cup in 1999 became a milestone in mass entertainment for women's sport more generally (Markovits and Hellerman 2003). Careful cultivation of the media, White House politicians (including President Clinton) and a fan base of young female players expanded the global popularity of women's football. While female migration to North American colleges would be a another project altogether, a worry about losing talent from Europe to North America was one of the primary factors in creating a degree of paid work for women football players in Europe.

In 2000, at a special round-table discussion with the national coaches of the European participants in the Los Angeles Women's World Cup, the implications of the tournament for European women's football was debated (UEFA 2000: 6). Chaired by Andy Roxburgh with Susanne Erlandsson, the meeting was attended by Frits Ahlstrom, Lars Arnesson, Gero Bisanz, Yuri Bystritsky, Des Casey, Marika Domaski-Lyfors, Karen Espelund, Carlo Facchin, Paul Højmose, Anne King, Marina Kravchenko, Tina Theune-Meyer, Tatiana Oberson, Guido Tognoni and Robin Russell. The coaches were concerned that the first three Women's World Cups in 1991, 1995 and 1999 had seen Europe begun to lag behind other confederations in spite of having more World Cup berths allocated to it than any other. Norway was considered the best European team in 1999, finishing fourth, but there was a consensus that UEFA needed to make some changes in order to regain its position as the leading confederation in women's football. On the whole, the coaches felt that the technical and tactical skills had improved significantly since Sweden 1995 and the first Olympic women's football tournament in Atlanta in 1996. Those in attendance felt that the Women's World Cup 1999 also marked a media breakthrough, as even people who were not normally interested in women's football had enjoyed following the matches. The success of the Women's World Cup 1999 consequently spurred a degree of inter-confederation rivalry: the fourth UEFA Conference on Women's Football in 2001, held at Oberhausen in Germany, was entitled «The Future of Women's Football in Europe: the Key Issues». Professionalisation began to include payment for national team players, as European nations sought to hold onto talented females who might be tempted to careers elsewhere.

The 2001 conference also reached a consensus on the need for continuing rapid development of European women's football, because elite competitions were limited to adults. Perhaps more importantly, an infrastructure of girls' football needed to be built up in every association, in an aim to keep female players active in football for longer. In many cases, very good players who could not make the national team had left football by the time they reached twenty-one years of age. The coaches believed a European club competition for women was extremely important in retaining playing talent. It was, they felt, increasingly difficult for a European national team to compete with Brazil, the USA or PR China. Europe had to build its own structures to prevent the «Atlantic Drift» of female European talent (Liston and Booth 2010: 1). This has consequently remained a concern of European national associations, UEFA and, to an extent, FIFA in the last decade. Also important has been the L-League, the Japanese women's equivalent of the men's «J» League, mainly providing semi-professional contracts since 1989. The league expanded from its original eight-team format to two divisions in 2004. By 2010/1 the first division had increased to ten clubs and the second division was further divided into an East and West group of six teams each.

The migration of athletes is a phenomenon dating back to the earliest days of sport itself and certainly in the wake of codification, modernization and industrialization. If new markets for female players are an important factor «pulling» them towards employment over increasingly wide geographical areas, «push» factors can be few lucrative contracts; a lack of prestige and a chance to experience new cultures through football. Being a female football player has not been an aspirational career path for many talented women athletes. We do not know how many women and girls have been lost to the sport because no viable living could be made from it. We do know, however, that for every Mia Hamm, Birgit Prinz or Marta there have been thousands for whom playing the game has cost much more than they will ever earn from it. What is especially important about these worldwide markets is that migrant female players are often the only professional players in the receiving club. They are significant exceptions that counterpoint the essentially amateur nature of the female game as a whole.

Only orthodoxy prevents female players earning a living in the more fully-developed extant male leagues. Mainly of these restraints are informal, rather than defensible by law, but it would be a very brave woman who had considerable financial backing, to take on the convoluted system to demonstrate her right to play in male leagues. She would also have to rely on being picked by a coach and negotiate the complexities of a professional subculture in which young boys have been seriously training to play as professional adults since they were eight or nine years old. Put simply, we are at a moment when women as individuals are pioneering and helping to construct the female professional leagues as a segmented employment market. While the male player is now an active agent in when, how and to whom his labour can be sold, the elite female footballer has the added burden of making «women's football» a viable commercial product. In the meantime, the professionalization of sport itself in the last fifty years has seen a rise both in specialization of function and increase in roles. We have moved away from the image of amateurs running 'backroom' functions of clubs at elite levels to professionals with training in the legal and business industries.

Administration in women's teams and leagues has struggled to catch up to meet the challenges of establishing a market-oriented commercial future. Although a cosmetics brand like Avon was able to endorse distance running as a way of selling products to female athletes in the 1970s, there has yet to be a comparable cultural change in football. Many sports brands rely on producing pink clothing and equipment as a concession to female players. It would perhaps take the endorsement of an aspirational, luxury brand to make women's football fashionable in Europe. Were Prada, Vivienne Westwood or Louis Vuitton to design women's football kits, this would mark a new moment in the cultural transfer of the game. Is the product to be understood in different terms than the men's game? What implications are there for UEFA's policy and role, and by extension, for the domestic and foreign policies of European nation-states more broadly? What does that mean for the way that football (with the same rules, same dress code, same subdisciplines in competition) is imagined, packaged and sold in its female form?

3. Conclusion

The academic framework has been taken from women's football, sporting migration, European football, the changing nature of European society and of the economic position of professional sport. It became apparent that women's football has received increased academic interest since my last work in this area in 2007 and that much of this has focussed on the question of nationalism and international player migration. I have continued my broadly qualitative approach as the topic is not about polar opposites of amateurism and professionalism. The evidence mainly suggests that semi-professionalism involves many shades of grey. For instance, the Frauen-Bundesliga has twelve clubs that are populated by «semi-professional and amateur» players (Hink 2009: 1). In another example, Røa, a Norwegian club who have consistently done well in European competition over the past ten years, offer their players contracts of between one and five years, with varying financial rewards few of which would enable players to sustain a living on football alone (Austad 2010).

Under FIFA rules a player is considered professional if they earn above their basic expenses from the game. Even if players spend most of their working lives playing it, most women are more accurately semi-professional, as they either work in addition to football to support themselves or are studying at the same time. Having highlighted the discrepancy between evidence in the public and private domain and «official» versions of events, I have used personal interviews, teleconferences, email communication, social media, electronic and paper-based questionnaires and attendance at proceedings (including UEFA-organised development events, sports contests, training sessions, promotional activities, academic conferences and media briefing exercises). Secondary data collection and meta-analysis took more time than originally envisaged due to the uneven datasets of the various UEFA and FIFA questionnaires, available only as hard-copy questionnaire returns. As suspected at the outset, getting returns to various requests for information remained the single most difficult aspect of the research process. It was especially difficult to obtain data to reflect the emerging eastern countries in top-flight competition. In spite of briefly meeting, and introducing my project to Zvezda club representatives in August 2010, for example, none of my subsequent enquiries to the Russian club had a response.

A major challenge then, was access to primary data across such a wide geographical spread in the timeframe of the project. However, some evidence of the European elite was identifiable in the final sixteen clubs of UEFA's Women's Champions League 2009/10 and in 2010/1. An emergent professional market was to be evident here and in the twelve-club Frauen-Bundesliga in Germany; the eight-squad Vrouwen Eredivisie in the Netherlands and the eight-team FA Women's Super League in England. However, there were problems and these leagues were not stable: after AZ and Willem II, FC Utrecht also discussed leaving the Eredivisie in the 2011/2 season. As the highest women's league in the Netherlands only five teams confirmed their intention to continue to play in 2012/3 at a meeting with the KNVB. Challenges included making the franchise more interesting to families by, for example, playing on Friday instead of Thursday; a free market for players and a new financial agreement between clubs. It is not yet clear at the time of writing what that free market or the financial arrangements might entail.

The FC Utrecht unease was particularly noteworthy as the team won both the Dutch Supercup and KNVB Cup in 2010. Bristol Women's Football Academy, one of the eight English Super League teams, then signed twenty-five year old international Anouk Hoogendijk as a star player. Hoogendijk left FC Utrecht after four seasons in March 2011, where she had also been Captain. As an ambassador for the sportswear company Nike, the midfielder had become one of the best-known women sports stars in the Netherlands with sixty caps for the national team. Two further British-born players who had worked in the Netherlands, Jess Fishlock, now aged 26, and Alex Culvin, aged 29, also signed for the Bristol squad. Jess is a Welsh international with 38 caps, who was controversially neglected in the squad for the British team at the London 2012 Games. Alex is English, previously playing for Leeds and Everton, and both transferred from Dutch club AZ Alkmaar. Like much of Europe, the story of women's soccer in the Netherlands has been «one of struggle for resources, acceptance, visibility, and legitimization with little result» (Knoppers and Anthonissen 2003: 13-33). We can be more optimistic as the women's national team of the Netherlands has continued to do well and growth in participation levels encouraging. However, controversy in 2008 over FC de Rakt players attempting to play in skirts to make the sport more 'feminine' do show how gender, sexuality, class and media images can remain challenging. Transfers within the EU have also meant the usual rehearsals of concerns about the influx of international players on the development of national team players in the Netherlands, Germany and England.

Germany became the most successful football nation in Europe after winning the world cup for the third time in 1990. In spite of full professionalism being allowed in male leagues only since 1972, the success of the national women's football team in the Women's World Cups of 2003 and 2007 make them the only country to have won both titles. The rapidity of the success of the German women's team requires analysis in its own right. After their relatively poor showing at Women's World Cup in 1999, where they lost 3-2 to the United States in the Quarter Finals, the team has thrived in a more competitive international situation. Examples from more eastern and central-European countries would also have strengthened the research. With more time and funding, the project would also have benefitted from looking more closely at the Iberian peninsular for three key reasons. First, because as the South Africa 2010 World Cup Champions, Spain are a growing force in world football and the women's team has more recently strengthened its international position. Secondly, the relationship between Portugal and Brazil is interesting because of the shared language and recent South American interest in the women's game. Thirdly, there is an under-developed literature on sport and religious conviction, in this case mainly Catholic countries and female participation, that the peninsular might be used to explore.

Besides the geographical variance, it was important to represent three main kinds of club ownership and practice in women's football. Examples of sports clubs include Røa, in Norway and Umeå IK from Sweden. Here football is one of many codes in a community-driven club that is not linked to a professional men's side. Both have been important at top-level European female competition, nevertheless. English club Arsenal, France's Olympique Lyonnais, FC Bayern Munich in Germany and AZ Alkmaar from the Netherlands, are all owned and run by professional men's clubs, or were until very recently. 1. FFC Turbine Potsdam and FCR 2001 Duisburg are proudly independent women's clubs as were Doncaster Belles at the outset. This affects the way that the organisations perceive their role in the community and in their own self-image. It also affects the way that clubs are imagined by the football authorities and the media.

In summary, the enlargement of the European project has corresponded with an increase in the popularity of playing football by women in many of the constituent countries, as a result of rulings in the late 1960s by

FIFA that national associations should take control of the female game. Individual interviews are therefore an essential method in exploring this period because relatively few women could earn a living from football at this time. This was followed by haphazard and varied degrees of integration until the FIFA Los Angeles Declaration in 1999 marked a new commitment on behalf of European governing bodies to the women's game. A degree of professionalization for some European women across the globe (but particularly in the United States) and for a number of international female players and coaches within the continent have been the main 'push' and 'pull' factors influencing migration.

FIFA and UEFA had, by this period, become themselves large bureaucratic organizations specializing in developing multiple competitions. Both Mikael Salzer, UEFA Head of Women's Competitions and Futsal, and Anne Vonnez, UEFA Head of Women's Competitions Division, made the point in our discussion about the increased bureaucratization of the governing bodies. Mikael had worked at the Swedish FA from 1974-6 and Anne has had a varied career at UEFA since 1998. As a consequence of this I have used material from the archives of the governing bodies and have benefitted from personal interviews with key players, coaches and administrators. I have also had to be necessarily selective in narrowing down the examples of competition to the FIFA Women's World Cup from 1991 to 2011, the new UEFA Women's Champions' League, which in 2010/1 was in its second season and, in England, the Super League launched in 2011. From these varied sources, this project as a whole explores the growth, specialized development and multiple aspects of professionalism in European women's football.

Micro, Meso and Macro Professionalism

I play football - and you? Ich spiele football - un du?

1. Introduction

An academic survey of European women's work spanning the last three centuries described this as a «hidden history» (Simonton 1998: 3). Professional women football players are part of this unknown story. Perhaps this is because of the significance of amateurism as a prevailing ethos in sport until the 1960s. Another newly-released academic survey by Deborah Simonton *Women in European Culture and Society* does makes reference to the rise of the female global sports star, beginning with Suzanne Lenglen's rather shocking appearance in short skirt, bandeau and sleeveless dress at Wimbledon in 1919 (2011: 386). There is, however, no mention of football until ten pages before the end of the book. Given that the subtitle of the book is *Gender, Skill and Identity from 1700*, we are reminded that football as a sport has often stood for modernity since its codification from 1863 onwards. Historic exclusion has made this especially the case for women football players. Nevertheless, it is often helpful sometimes to look at the wider context of female patterns of employment to help us understand what happens in sport.

Often described as a product of so-called «second wave» feminism of the 1970s playing football seemed to combine the invasion of traditionally «male spaces» such as the pitch and the locker room with signs of an assertive physicality on behalf of women with enough stamina to compete in a contact sport for ninety minutes. However, this can be overly deterministic, in that my previous research indicated that most of the women playing at this time did not define themselves as feminists or as politically active. They simply had been introduced to football, enjoyed playing and did what they had to do in order to participate at whatever level of intensity they chose (Williams 2003: 24). We also know that women have played football for over a century, so the story of increased female forcefulness and resilience in the 1970s seems to be misleading. After discussion with colleagues who specialise in the analysis of migration, I have conceptualized the period between 1971 and 2011 as having three overlapping stages of professionalism: these are micro, meso and macro (Agergaard and Bothelo 2010). It is important to emphasize however, that these phases describe a growing infrastructure of opportunities for women generally, but that cross-European variation in the developing and core countries for women's football also complicates the picture. I am not suggesting that we have reached a phase of widespread female employment in football by using the phrase macro professionalism. Rather, conditions are potentially more favourable and diverse now than at any previous time in history.

While we can be encouraged by an emergent professionalization with structural and socio-cultural conditions that differ significantly at international level from 1971, in some European countries, football for women is still neglected in civil society and excluded from sport and economic support systems. The organization of semi-professional leagues consequently sees the current opportunities for women as some way off full-professionalism. This cautionary note about the use of the three-part model should also contextualise it as a point of departure to stimulate further debate. I nevertheless intend to move from micro professionalism (where important individuals can be identified); to meso professionalism (with the establishment of greater international opportunities presented by transnational competition and the creation of a Women's World Cup); to macro professionalism (with a multiplicity of international competitions and tournaments where women might showcase their football skill in order to obtain employment). Few women earn a full-time living-wage entirely from their football playing career in Europe. However, the ancillary occupations around the sport (coaching, sport development, public relations, administration, physiotherapy and sports psychology, for instance) enable women increasingly to support themselves from football related-earnings. It would be easy, and of limited value, to be distracted by taking Premiership or Serie A wages and contracts as comparators in talking about female professionalism. Football is as varied and transient an occupation for many men who work in it as it can be for women. The qualitative data highlights some areas for future research. Some of these have policy and applied implications, for instance, those that could be addressed to prevent a loss of female expertise and talent from the game as the structures around professionalism continue to develop.

Football and its academic study have changed considerably in the last sixty years. In 1994 two of the pioneers of labour migration in sport, John Bale and Joseph Maguire, noted that the movement of workers was gathering pace and spanning more widespread geographical areas for an increasing number of sub-disciplines (1994: 10). Female clubs and leagues are important drivers of migration and have their own identities. As Bale and Maguire indicated, we are not just concerned with the actions of individuals but also «We are dealing with ethnoscapes, and technoscapes, financescapes and ideoscapes» (1994: 7). Despite this growing academic treatment, even today, there is little literature on migration concerning women's sports.

This is itself changing with more cutting-edge research in sport generally, as the recent Oxford University symposium on Women's Sport in Africa evidenced, with papers on running, netball and football (Sikes 2011). Women's football is now a growing academic subject from a variety of disciplinary approaches examining processes of globalization, commercialization and professionalization. A paradoxical situation has developed whereby employment opportunities for women are now emerging but the product «women's football» remains intangible to prospective sponsors. Because FIFA, UEFA and national associations struggle to define what advertisers call the Unique Selling Point (USP) of the women's game in relation to the men's there are, in general, poor economic conditions for leagues, clubs and female footballers alike. In the sections that follow I have included direct quotations from players I have spoken to, and have also differentiated their longer comments by font style. My reasons are three-fold. First, the women cited here have collaborated with me by giving their time and expertise to the project and the diversity of their experience is one of the key findings of the research-process. Second, their interpretation of events is little-known and deserves a wider recognition. As people who have sustained careers and, in many cases, formed their own opportunities, this aspect of women's work, let alone of sports history, is significant. To this end, I have kept the original style of conversation and punctuation unless the meaning was not clear. I then checked through ambivalent sections in my printed version of our conversation with the respondent. Thirdly, I wanted to differentiate my analysis of their careers with their own words. They have all seen drafts of the work before publication and we discussed my interpretation on given issues. It is a mark of their considerable generosity that players who do not agree with me were still prepared to contribute their stories. It is worth reinforcing the point that the arguments are mine alone and do not represent the views of players, unless explicitly referenced.

2.   Micro Professionalism: Pioneering Individual Women Football Players

An international network of women's football existed well before the mid 1960s, while into the 1980s UEFA/ FIFA were still debating whether there was sufficient depth in competitive women's football to host «official» tournaments. The careers of some of the pioneering women of the 1970s and 1980s show how a nascent professionalism developed first outside, then inside the structures of the sports governing bodies. It took radical and forward-looking people in different countries to get things organised, and especially so in Italy. It is clear that there were outstanding women players at this time, and some evidence of strength in depth. The case studies begin with Sue Lopez who was born in 1945 and briefly played in Italy as an interruption to her career with Southampton Women's Football Club from 1966 to 1986. During this time Sue played in many overseas tournaments; evidence of movement, rather than migration in women's football. In 1971 Sue Lopez spent a season helping Roma to win the Italian national cup and they also finished second in the league. It is clear that Lopez moved and found accommodation in Italy, arranged daily living conditions and therefore migrated. Her motivation was primarily for competitive reasons. Her observations tell us about the wider standard of play at this time. This raises questions of how some elite women players developed their skills given the lack of infrastructure for women's football. Sue Lopez also suggested that Italy was the most important European country for the development of professional women's soccer during this period, in spite of some talented English players.

Case study one: Sue Lopez, the temporary football migrant

I have known Sue Lopez since first contacting her about my PhD research in 1998 and to the extent that our paths have crossed occasionally since. Most of what follows is taken from her response to a questionnaire on 30 December 2010, developed by several follow up phone conversations and emails. Sue Lopez first began playing in the South Hants Ladies' Football Association League created in 1966 by women inspired by England's 1966 World Cup victory. Each club affiliated for the equivalent today of 50 pence and player registration cost 35 pence. From these localised circumstances, Lopez and her team-mates had their eyes on European football. The Royex team, for whom she first played, were an office team based in the Royal Exchange Assurance depot in the town. They soon changed their name to Real FC in 1967-8. The Deal international women's football tournament, first held in 1967, grew to a larger 32 team event the next year and had 52 entries in 1969. Through this competition, Lopez became aware of more European teams: these included Sparta Praha and Slavia Kaplice from Czechoslovakia and a side from Vienna. Cambuslang Hooverettes, the Scottish champions from Glasgow also participated.

In the 1970 Deal tournament, Cambuslang lost to Southampton Women's Football Club on penalties, to give the team for which Lopez now played its first title. Combined with the Butlins Cup (which was jointly organised by the holiday camp chain; the commercial television channel, ITV and the newspaper *The Daily Mirror*) the Deal tournament encouraged enough domestic interest to create the Women's Football Association (WFA) in England. A Women's Football Association club affiliation fee was set at 15 pence. Transfers of players between clubs cost 12 pence. As there was no official England women's team, Lopez first travelled to the Fédération Internationale Européenne de Football Féminin (FIEFF) tournament in 1969 to discover how advanced women's football was in Europe; how it was played and in what circumstances it could flourish. The following transcript is Sue Lopez's description of how the tournament led to her move to Italy:

> In 1968 there were several active women's football teams in large cities such as Rome (Roma, Lazio), Florence, Turin, Milan, Naples, Genoa, Piacenza as well as Sardinia (Cagliari). Next year there was a championship with ten teams, and a national game against the Czechs. So by the time of the Turin tournament in November 1969, women's football was being taken seriously in Italy; hence their national team was well

provided for. By appearance and conduct, on and off the pitch, the French and Danish also looked serious about the game, too. Despite being a group of players from two or three clubs who hadn't played together before, «England» certainly performed in a competent manner, but by comparison, we looked very much the «poor relations».

The English team for the 1969 tournament had the bare basics. The guy, Harry Batt manager of Chiltern Valley women's club, who had received the invite to this tournament from FIEFF brought a second-hand used red kit, red socks, white shorts – most of us brought our own shorts! We all wore our own tracksuits – some sewed on little Union Jack flags to give a sense of national pride. The Italians and French had quality-looking national team replica kit and the Danish wore a «professional» looking all-white strip. Most of them were from the Danish Femina club, who wore white, so maybe it was their kit. Harry and his wife had a First Aid kit, but I can't vouch for their medical knowledge.

Food, accommodation and travel in Italy was very good. All was free of charge, including travel to Italy (by train). Training facilities were better than most of us experienced at home. Our match versus Denmark was played at Valle d'Aosta, near the accommodation we shared with the Danes. The Italy versus France match was at Novara. The Final and third place play-off was at the outstanding Stadio Comunale in Turin attended by 10,000 spectators. In the Final Italy beat Denmark 3-1, and we beat France 2-0 there to take third place. I scored one of the goals, and captained the team again. By far, this was the most professional atmosphere I'd played in. Even the Aosta local pitch was very good, but the Turino Stadio Comunale was at least similar to a good Championship or Division One ground in England. The *Corriere dello Sport* cuttings of the tournament illustrate how important women's football was to the Italians, way back then. This was serious, comprehensive coverage, with super photos. Matches were played on good pitches, especially the final in Torino.

As we were accommodated with the Danes and several spoke good English, we found that they also had the basis of some organisation in their country. Their better players were looking to play professionally, and after the tournament two of the Danish team, including Maria Sevcikova (who was, in fact, a Czech citizen) stayed on with me in Turin to trial for Real Torino. I was feted by the organisers as one of the top players in the tournament, and was very happy to be a guest of Real Torino for a few days, along with Maria. Our team-mates went straight home after the final games. I returned in March 1970 with Dot Cassall to play in a trial friendly game against Yverdon (a Lausanne team) at the Stadio Communale again, and we won 10-0. I scored 5 goals. By this time, the English and Italian national Press was regularly reporting about my possible move to Italy.

After I returned home to consider the move, Roma started phoning me and inviting me there, which of course I subsequently accepted. Torino had not been very specific about the deal, whereas Roma were very persuasive regarding accommodation, travel, and they were at the time quite a successful club. For Roma, Medri, the skipper and centre back Lucia Gridelli were international players. The team played a passing game of football and some had outstanding ball control. This was probably another reason I liked it Italy, though some of the Southampton teams I played in were very skilled, which is why there were always five or so in the national team. Our opponents in Italy also had some good international players of course; especially our main rivals, Piacenza, who won the league when I was there, and we came second. I scored in a crucial game against them but we lost 2-1. I think it was Piacenza that originally wanted to sign me, or was it Bergamo? It would have been interesting to discover how Italian players became so good. The Federazione Femminile Italiana Gioco Calcio (FFIGC) started a league in 1970 with nine, then ten teams, and in 1971 it grew to fourteen. In December 1972 it seems that the Federazione Italiana Calcio Femminile (FICF) and FFIGC united and there was a Serie A and Serie B League system.

I agreed with the impression from the Danes (and Czech) that Italy offered the opportunity to play competitive full-time football to a good standard in an organised national league at no cost to us. I felt respected by my manager, trainer and colleagues, and fans. I was absolutely amazed that the national sports paper *Corriere dello Sport* reported all our matches in a full, serious and respectful way. They had a dedicated sports reporter in Gianni Bezz. He was a charming man who treated us with great respect whenever we met him at matches and he attended most of them. And of course, it was an attractive country in which to live. I never knew what kind of money was offered to players at Roma or elsewhere. I was very happy to be a full-time player. I had accommodation within walking distance of Mira and Franco Bellei's apartment at Ostia Lido, a short train journey from the centre of Rome. I took my main meal of the day with the Bellei family and they arranged breakfast at a local café. I lodged in a one-room apartment with Gibus. Monika Karner, an Austrian striker lodged at the Bellei's where she occasionally assisted them with certain off the field club duties.

At the end of the season, we had an all-expenses paid trip to Bangkok. Roma had been there before, too. We played at the Palasuka National Stadium after a men's «rubber» match with two arch rival men's teams, including the local champions. Our first match was against a local Bangkok select boys' team. We lost 8-1 as the boys, who were all under eighteen, were fitter and stronger than us. We played another game two days later against a less good boys' team but I can't remember the score. The price of tickets ranged from 15 to 30 baht. On arrival at Bangkok airport we were received by our local hosts, and each garlanded with flowers beside the plane, and then again inside the airport. Photos were taken by the local press of our visit and two matches were reported in the Bangkok Post. We stayed in a first class hotel, and were escorted on a tour of the city, to temples and the Floating Market, and an official visit to a local children's hospital.

On return to Rome, I went home early in the New Year. At the time I was also being lured away to one or two of the northern Italian teams for the new season (spring time), but I was also being told by the WFA that players playing abroad wouldn't be considered for the impending first ever official England team, so I didn't return. Also, my colleagues at Southampton were keen for me to return as there was a national Cup impending. I realised playing in Italy that I was one of the best players, and as a successful striker, very valued, and respected by everyone I encountered – unlike in England sometimes. There were absolutely no hassles and I loved the Italian way of life. So, it was a very difficult decision not to return. But I was patriotic and very keen to see the game develop here in England, and I believed it would do so more quickly than it did. Also, I'd been a big football fan of English men's football since about the age of 9 or 10 when my grandfather would take me to some Saints matches, and Mum would buy me a football magazine to feed my love of the game, and she was a big fan, too. I guess if I'd known how slow it would be to develop in this country, and without the threat of a ban if I played abroad, I would have returned to Italy, maybe to a bigger club in the north, and learnt the language, and made a career there. But I wouldn't have played for England, presumably, nor had the thrill of winning eight FA Women's Cup Finals.

But women's football was still not being taken seriously in England and I can only say that my whole football experience in Italy was enjoyable and positive. By contrast in England it was a constant battle to have the game recognised as a serious female sport, and dependent on players paying their own way for most things. Belatedly, I realised that the pleasure of playing in Italy was not to have all the distractions that players had to put up with here. Despite an England team starting, there weren't any official tournaments like now. And the unofficial ones were soon banned. Also, the local and national political battles impacted on players.

In concluding this case study, we can see that Lopez was careful to distance herself from the players in the Italian leagues who reportedly earned upwards of £40 a week at the time. Lopez was careful to emphasise that she was an amateur (drawing only living and travelling expenses) in case she was banned by the FA or professionalism. Even with this scrupulous attitude, there were clearly material benefits, such the trip to Bangkok and a wider sense of being respected. Combined media and business interests were the primary «pull» factors to encourage players, spectators and commercial prospects to Italy. Along with Sue Lopez, English players like Dorothy «Dot» Cassall also went to Italy and Joan Clements had one or two games for Roma but neither stayed for a whole season. I do not propose here to focus on what might be classified as «curiosity tourism» which is more evidence of player movement than migration. Lopez was by no means alone in experiencing a club or country dilemma that limited her ability to earn a living from the game in which she excelled. The example highlights structural factors including lack of national team opportunities; the antipathy of national associations and media scepticism over female footballers' credibility as the most significant drivers to «push» players from England to Italy.

Sue Lopez went on to contribute a leading role in the administration of the WFA and was an important player in the England team. She made twenty-two appearances, alongside Janey Bagguley, Syliva Gore, Wendy Owen and Lynda Hale until she retired from international football in 1979 (Owen 2005). Notable players Debbie Bampton, Gill Coulthard and Marianne Spacey were to follow. One of seven women to hold the highest A Licence coaching certificate in 1998, Lopez briefly coached the Wales national side. Subsequently, Sue Lopez has earned a living from her coaching, continued as an academic and teacher of physical education. Due to the changing employment sector in women's football, Lopez has negotiated a career path that has often involved multiple roles. She summarises her career since 1997 in the following way:

> Since writing my book, I left my role as Coaching and Development Officer for Hants FA, where I organised and delivered FA Licence course for the county, and in 1998 at the same time ran the newly-evolved post of Director of Saints Girls Centre of Excellence. In 2000 I joined Southampton FC full time as Head of Women's football, running the Premier League women's team, Reserve team, Academy, and Centre of Excellence until the whole women's programme was cut when Saints men were relegated in 2005. During my time in that role 27 girls were in the England Talent Identification group; several went on to represent England at various youth levels and one became a full England player. I then became a part time Tutor of FA courses for Hants FA and local higher education establishments. I have received several honours since: the 1999 *Sunday Times* Sportswoman of the Year, Coach of the Year; 2000 MBE for service to women's football; 2004 National Football Museum Hall of Fame - the third female inductee and in 2006 an Honourary Doctorate from Southampton University for services to women's football.

For much of her active playing career Lopez was enormously respected and the same has been true of her vocation for coaching. Without considering the tensions and challenges of how one of the most successful women players of her time negotiated foreign labour markets, we might also risk a rather skewed version of football's past. The organization of the Italian leagues at this time shows a degree of business and organisational sophistication. However, to appreciate how significant the Italian situation was, the next case study looks at a player who moved from Scotland to play in Italy at the age of eighteen and kept her primary residence in the country until she was forty five.

Case study two: Rose Reilly-Peralta, the long-term migrant

I interviewed Rose Reilly by phone and the evidence that she has been able to provide was less detailed than Sue Lopez's memories. Much of the documentation of her playing career remains in storage in Italy. Because she was unable to complete a questionnaire, the following summary of her career is in the third person, transcribed from our conversations. Rose Reilly was born in Kilmarnock in 1955 and played for Stewarton United as a young girl, with scouts from the professional men's side, Celtic, remarking her striking ability, though she could not be signed for an apprenticeship. A natural athlete, at the age of sixteen Rose was chosen to represent Scotland at the Commonwealth Games in the pentathlon. However, the amateur nature of track and field athletics meant that she would not have been able to earn a living from it and so she concentrated on her football skills. She played for Stewarton and Thistle Ladies Football Club until 1972 when she briefly transferred for a year to Westhorn United.

Having been involved in trials to form an unofficial Scottish women's national team to play in tournaments in 1966, 1967 and 1969 Reilly became aware that moving to mainland Europe would further her football career. Her subsequent list of achievements is astonishing, considering the obstacles faced by female footballers in the early 1970s. At the age of 17 Reilly had a trial for Reims in France where she played for six months on a professional contract involving basic pay, accommodation and travel expenses. At the age of 18, Reilly signed for A. C. F. Milan. Professional club and amateur country tension surfaced in 1972, when an official Scotland women's team was created, with a volunteer male manager lacking coaching qualifications. Having been used to a more organised and professional approach in Italy, Reilly, along with Edna Nellis and Elsie Cook, complained about the lack of rigour. In response, all three were banned from football for life by the Scottish Football Association (SFA). When the SFA relented two years later, Reilly became one of the more senior international players with ten caps. However, Reilly experienced more success, after taking official Italian citizenship, with the unofficial Italian national women's team. She would go on to become an unofficial world cup winner as their captain and lead striker.

Rose Reilly transferred between teams in order to improve her prospects while in Italy and played for Milan from 1973-7; Catania 1978-9; Lecce 1980-3; Trani 1984-6; Napoli 1986-8 and Florence 1988-90. Eventually retiring aged forty, after playing for Bari and Agliana in her later years, Reilly became a well known enough football player to appear on chat shows and to endorse the health benefits of ice cream. In all, Rose Reilly played in teams that won eight Italian women's league titles; four national cup competitions and she had a personal highlight of scoring forty-five goals in the 1980/1 season. Reilly had also previously been the leading goal scorer with forty-three in the league for Milan. The number of transfers experienced by Rose Reilly made this a somewhat peripatetic lifestyle and one consequence of this was the challenge in storing personal memorabilia. Other difficulties included loneliness and long hours in airports and hotels. In the 1978/9 season Reilly helped win championship titles in both Italy and France, playing for Lecce on a Saturday night and then flying to France to play for Reims on Sunday afternoons.

Reilly was more thoroughly integrated with Italian everyday life than Sue Lopez. This included including learning the language, which she said was partly motivated by being the only English speaking player in a team and in part as a way of following football matches in the *Gazzetta dello Sport*. Not a natural student, she determined to learn a different word each day and became fluent. She reported to me that other players on the Italian women's national side would sing «God Save the Queen» during the national anthems before matches in order to make her feel at home, in spite of her unsuccessful attempts to teach them «O Flower of Scotland». Rose was capped twenty two times for Italy and scored thirteen goals. As captain, Reilly was voted best player in the Italian World Cup team that beat the USA by three goals to one in the unofficial women's world cup final hosted by the Asian Ladies Football Association in 1983. Winning the Golden Boot and scoring in the final, Reilly was also voted the most valuable player of the tournament.

Between 1984 and 1986, Reilly was the only player on the board at Trani, drawing in about £1,000 a month, with free accommodation provided, plus sponsorship from local companies and complimentary sports clothing. She also ran a small sports shop in the town to supplement her income. Rose married her football coach, Norberto Peralta at the age of forty with whom she had a daughter, Megan who is also fluent in Italian. Norberto was a doctor from Argentina by profession who had migrated to Italy and volunteered as physiotherapist for the local football team. After remaining in Italy until 2001, the family returned to Scotland to nurse Rose's mother who was by then elderly and frail. Rose Reilly was inducted Scottish Sports Hall of Fame in March 2007, also becoming the first woman in the Scottish Football Hall of Fame later in the year, ranked alongside the likes of Alan Hansen and Gordon Strachan. At the time of writing she is currently still the only female player to be honoured in this way.

Case study three: Vera Pauw, the European internationalist

The following summary is based on telephone and email discussions with Vera Pauw, a UEFA Women's Football Committee member and one of the most respected coaches, who has also been able to earn a sustained living from her football-related employment. Recognised by FIFA and UEFA for her work, most of what follows is a summary of her career achievements, with some excerpts from a questionnaire. Vera Pauw was born in Amsterdam in 1963 and quickly developed a dual role as player and coach/ technical development specialist. By 1983 the defender had been selected for the first of eighty nine national team appearances but the Netherlands did not qualify for the final tournament of a World Cup or European Championship during her career. In 1986 the football association of the Netherlands (KNVB) assisted Pauw with experience to get her UEFA «A» Licence coaching qualification in 1986 and she became more involved in coaching and sports policy. As a staff tutor of the KNVB football development policy, Pauw developed and delivered coaching and tutor courses for adults and children. From 1986 onwards Vera worked more and more outside of Europe on FIFA sponsored technical courses, seminars, lectures and in privately owned soccer camps in the US, Canada, Africa and Asia. She retired as an international player in 1998 but her coaching expertise has made her one of the most significant figures for the development of women's football world-wide.

She is also one of the few Dutch women to have played football professionally. The Federazione Italiana Giuoco Calcio Femminile (FIGCF) affiliated to the Italian FA in 1980. Some of the competition between the leagues that Sue Lopez experienced during her time as a player in Italy were resolved by officially recognising only the FIGCF. Vera played professionally in Italy for Modena FC for the 1988/9 season, when she earned the equivalent of 1,500 Euros today, in addition to being provided with an apartment; car; six flight tickets; food and training assistance. Living in the country allowed her to study the Italian language which she enjoyed. She married another football coach, Bert van Lingen who worked as assistant manager of Rangers in Glasgow from 1998 when Pauw became manager and technical director of women's football in Scotland. In 2004 Pauw took up a similar role with the Netherlands and led her home country to the semi-final of the UEFA Women's Euro tournament in 2009. In April 2011 she became coach of the Russia women's national football team and is now a technical director.

Reflecting on her motivations to play professionally in Italy, Vera said that she was drawn by:

> Recognition and competitiveness, the chance to be able to live by playing my sport at the highest level. Later the value of status showed how important this decision was and this remains the same now. At the time, I never realized what «side effects» it would bring, but it has influenced my total career. With the exception of the year in Italy, I had always worked to supplement my income and because I enjoyed the game. This included volunteering as a coach. Now, the Dutch National Team have professional-style preparation without the pay. The difference between club level and representative football is the main area of development. In my time the difference was massive. Now the club level is preparation for the National team, but in my time as a player club-level experience was a necessity. If I had been given the choice, we would have stepped out of the league to prepare with the National Team only.

Case Study four: Gao Hong, the elite retired-player migrating into Europe

The following summary is an interview conducted with Gao Hong, the former PR China national team goalkeeper, in Stratford Upon Avon during 2010 when she was studying for coaching qualifications in England. Hong was born in 1967. At school she mainly played table tennis, gymnastics and basketball at the Sadie sports school. However, she was perceived to be under-height to be a good basketball player. She consequently began work, aged fourteen, at a yarn factory in the Mongolian region of Huheaote which had a mainly female workforce and where she continued to play basketball at an amateur level. When she was eighteen the Diermas Fangzhi factory established a women's football team and, though she was not keen to join initially, after three months she made the Nei Menggu (inner Mongolia) provincial team as goalkeeper. The team competed for the national championship and Gao was offered a place at a sports school,

with a standard package of reimbursement from the provincial government including a salary, accommodation, training and food, plus a win
bonus.

Not the most enthusiastic participant in training by her own admission, Gao claims to have had «one great game» in the Mongolian national
championship, though this is likely to be modesty. As a result, four provincial teams made an approach with improved contracts and she chose
Shan Xi over Beijing because she was over-awed by the scale of city life
in the latter. Nicknamed «grandma» for her supposedly advanced age, she
then sat on the bench for four years. It looked as though her career would
stall at this stage in spite of playing against boys' teams and an intensive
training regime that saw her technique improve considerably.

In 1989 thirty women's senior teams competed for the national championship of the PR China and at this tournament Gao Hong won an award
for the best goalkeeper in the competition. This transition to national squad
selection, and then to be the first-pick goalkeeper for the team was a difficult one personally, in terms of new expectations about her performance
and the isolation of competing with others on the same side for selection.
In addition to the national team, Hong played for the Ban Qiu Dian Qi
company team in south China. This was necessary because those sports
not in the Olympic charter did not receive the same level of provincial
funding as those covered by it and football, as had been said, was not to be
included until 1996. At company level, Hong was funded for three years
as a star player but the training was more intense and challenging. After
doing some training at the Beijing Sports University in physical education, particularly at elementary school level, a 1993 Asian championship
competition led to Hong's first trans-national migration. In 1994 the Taka-
lazaka team from Japan signed her, mainly at that stage for the second
team, on a salary of $3,000 a month, tax-free, plus accommodation.

The period between 1994 and 1996 was consequently a turning point in
Gao Hong's career because she worked with a very professional set-up under a German coach she called Mister Hermedo (she could not remember
his first name). In 1995, for the second Women's World Cup in Sweden,
Gao was re-selected for the PR China national team at the relatively late
age of twenty-eight. This re-call saw a new confidence in the team and its
preparation; including the use of visualization techniques, better nutrition-
al preparation and positive psychological development for three months
before the competition. However, of the four possible goalkeepers, only

two were expected to join the squad. Hong recalled being supported by her club coach who flew out to see her when she made the squad as second-choice goalkeeper but did not start the third game against Denmark. The quarter-final match against Sweden was therefore a big moment for the team as a whole since in the 1991 tournament China had lost to them by a one goal at that same stage. Having been selected, Gao Hong announced to the squad that she was ready to lead «My Generation» and saved two penalties to become feted by journalists as the «smiling goalkeeper» who was a powerhouse in her team. This legend grew in 1996 at the Olympic competition, when some assessed her to be the best female goalkeeper in the world. From 1996 to 1999 she had the possibility to emigrate to Canada for a college-based career. An alternative offer was a move back to Japan for a salary of $7,000 to play professionally there.

In 1997 however, she chose to return to PR China on a lower salary, of about $700 per month, because she missed the country and thought she would have a better chance of selection for the national team. Gao Hong nevertheless felt that she was mainly a domestic star, with an outgoing and boyish style, until her surprise selection for the FIFA All-Star team to play in the approach to Women's World Cup 1999. International media interest in she and Sun Wen increased again shortly after by the 2000 Olympic competition. In 2001 Gao moved to play for the New York Power team in the Women's United Soccer Association for two and a half seasons. A half season for the Washington Freedom followed. Having realized a child-hood ambition to emigrate to the United States, the suspension of trading of WUSA in 2003 meant that she, and many others lost their right to work in North America. Gao then joined the non-profit organization, Right to Play, in PR China for three years. As someone who had experienced an in-creased spiritual awareness and gender mentoring commitment, the Right to Play initiative involved using sport as a development tool in the lives of women and young girls. This was followed by a year at York University in Toronto, Canada.

Gao went to Women's World Cup in 2007 as a commentator but did not enjoy media work and sought instead to develop a coaching career. She identified European influences as particularly significant in making the transition to coaching, on her retirement from international football, par-ticularly those from Denmark, Norway and England. Consequently when I interviewed her in 2010 she was in England on a student visa study-ing a coaching course at Worcester University, while also getting experience at Birmingham City Ladies' FC and had worked with Hope Powell and Maureen (Mo) Marley at Loughborough University. In concluding, I asked why England was her current base, given Gao's multi-lingual and varied skill-set. In response she answered simply: «To experience the British football culture: to be in a country (sic) where football matters very much, every day». In concluding the micro case studies of this chapter, we can see that for each of these very different women football has mattered very much, if not every day, then for enough of their lives that they have moved across the world in search of opportunities to play and earn a living from the game.

3.   Meso Professionalism: Club Football, Growing Internationalism and World Championships

The decisions leading to the establishment of a Women's Euro competition, with an inaugural tournament held between 1982 and 1984, provides a way into the historical context of meso professionalism. It has already been said that the original sixteen-team tournament sharpened trans-European rivalries and provided important precursors to wider UEFA and FIFA control and development of the women's game. Confederation-organized international tournaments marked a degree of jurisdiction over, and promotion of, elite female play. England lost to Sweden in the first women's Euro event before Norway went on to win in 1987 and 1993, while the tournament has been dominated by Germany in more recent times. Scandinavia and Germany seem to have been at the heart of the development of the women's game in Europe, while Italy, France and England also appear central. Whether these countries have also provided core-centres for employability, drawing in players from the European periphery and beyond needs further investigation still. So club-based competition in Europe was significant in this next phase of development, because many of those women playing at elite level traversed the unofficial semi-professional subculture outside of national association control before playing in sanctioned leagues and national squads.

More significantly, key individuals have gone on to act as players, coaches and managers in the current systems. The point can be succinctly illustrated by looking at the golden boot winners for Euro tournaments across its history: Anne Mäkinen (2005); Hanna Ljungberg (2001); Carolina Morace (1997); Birgit Prinz (1995); Hege Riise (1993); Silvia Neid (1991); Doris Fitschen (1989); Heidi Støre (1987) and Pia Sundhage (1984). Sundhage, for example, coached the US women's national team from 2008-12 before returning to manage her native Sweden; Sylvia Neid coached the German women's national team (managed by Doris Fitschen) and Carolina Morace has coached both the Italian and the Canadian women's national team, in addition to earning a living as a television presenter. These women were important mentors and ambassadors in the macro phase of professionalism. I have tried to contact each to participate in this research but was not successful by the time of writing-up. I would hope therefore to extend the use of case studies in the previous section in developing this research to include more data from this group of significant individuals. An online European football Hall of Fame, which included profiles of women players, would help to focus and promote their wider visibility.

By the time of the first Women's World Cup in PR China 1991, female player migration saw gradually increasing fluxes into, and out of, Europe. Football at this moment perhaps assumed more globalized characteristics as the female population became more properly incorporated into the remit of the football bureaucracies. While the percentage of top players who left the developing countries of women's football to play in overseas leagues can be indicated as small, from the micro examples previously described, migration (albeit temporary and sometimes for no more than a season) was undoubtedly stimulated by the introduction of more competition and a growing internationalism. In 1985 UEFA surveyed national associations for a second time about the status of women's football in their country.

Table n°1: Women playing football and women's club in Europe (1985)

Country	Players	Clubs
Austria	1,000	59
Belgium	3,500	150
Czechoslovakia	800	22
Denmark	30,000	1,500
England	10,000	272
Finland	2,157 women, 1,207 girls	103 women, 74 girls
France	27,000	920
FR Germany	374,694	2,455 women and 975 girls
German DR	4,000	221 but 50 regularly engaged teams
Hungary	280	6 in regular competition
Iceland	2,300	42
Italy	10,000	406
Luxembourg	207	5
Netherlands	24,267 women, 11,014 girls	2,500
Norway	41,000 (over 10 years of age)	1,779
Northern Ireland	200	10
Portugal	743	41
Poland	650	16
Republic of Ireland	1,680	720
Russia	1,475	775
Spain	1,256	56
Sweden	37,577 (over 15 years of age)	1,500
Switzerland	2,200	94
Wales	80	5
Yugoslavia	3,000	20

Source: UEFA 1985 Survey on women's football

Though this information has to be read in the wider context of a primary concern with the number of women players, it does give us a snapshot of European-wide perceptions of the game in the thirty-four national associations affiliated to UEFA that year (UEFA Minutes of Committee on Women's Football 1985: 1-3). For example, the national association in Albania, Bulgaria, Cyprus, Greece, Liechtenstein, Malta, Romania, Turkey and the USSR declared that there was no women's football in their country. Cross-European comparison became an increasingly-used tool to measure the overall rise in participation from this date onwards. Whilst the statistics do not represent either the «facts» or the «reality» of female participation in any straightforward way, they do tell a story of institutionalized surveillance and development that increased from the early 1980s onwards.

This was not a geographically even, sustained or steady rise though. A report on the final round of the European Women's Championship hosted by Italy in 1993 summarised more negative feedback than positive (UEFA Women's Football Committee 1993: 2). The report, edited by Christophe von Wattenwyl, found the provisions for competition between Denmark, Germany, Italy and Norway underwhelming. The Press service was deemed inadequate for overseas media and it was recommended that a UEFA press representative should attend in future. The marketing concept of the tournament was reconsidered. Sports centres had been used as changing rooms for competitions and a lack of exclusivity for players had led to confusion. Future recommendations included that each delegation should have an official to help and accreditation should be given. An opening and closing ceremony, sufficient team accommodation provided at a hotel or sports school and financial accounts were other priorities. Basic organizational elements were somewhat ad hoc into the 1990s.

The period also saw an increasing focus on competitions for young women. We know that professionalism has driven the specialisation of football skills at increasingly young ages in male football. So a concern with age is part of wider patterns of professionalism. The following two tables give results from questionnaires on how many licensed Under 20 and Under 16 female players there were in national associations from 1993. The twenty-eight responding national associations (of the forty-four who were affiliated to UEFA at the time) were divided into a table of those with fewer than 1,000 registered players in total and those with more.

Table n°2: National Associations with fewer than 1,000 registered Under 20 players (1993)

Country	Under 16	Under 20	Total
Austria	0	500	500
Belarus	13	78	91
Bulgaria	16	29	45
Croatia	24	22	46
Faroe Islands	270	460	730
Greece	152	403	555
Latvia	150	18	168
Liechtenstein	20	20	40
Northern Ireland	40	90	130
Poland	120	210	330
Portugal	77	205	282
Romania	35	341	376
Scotland	500	200	700
Ukraine	81	157	238

Source: UEFA 1993 Survey on Girls and Women's Football

Some associations were targeted as requiring extra help to develop participation by UEFA and FIFA, but the exercise was also used to gauge a level of interest in female youth football in terms of planning for more competitions. The national associations who had more than 1,000 registered U20 players are listed in the following table. Again, there was more widespread interest than had been anticipated.

A subsequent Working Group on Women's Football met in May 1994 at the Hotel Doyle Montrose Dublin, led by Karen Espelund, Per Ravn Omdal and Maria Theresa Grau. The committee concluded that the first UEFA Under 18 female youth tournament should be staged without any subsidies whatsoever to gauge the financial burdens for each participating association (UEFA Minutes of Working Group 1994: 2). It was acknowledged that many associations would not be able to compete under these conditions, however, financial considerations took precedence over development issues. For example, costs for the UEFA Women's Championship in 1991/3 subsidies had been CHF 700,000 for the qualifying rounds to produce an overall small net profit. Meanwhile the male Under 16 youth tournament and Under 18 youth championship for the 1992/3 seasons had each been supported by CHF 1 million subsidies. At the most recent European Women's Championship meanwhile, statistics had shown that 15% of players had been under the age of 20; 40% between 20 and 25, and 45% had been over 25 years old. So gradually the focus began to shift from the existence of a national league and a senior female representative team in each country to look at a proliferation of competition, increasing specialization at a young age and a move towards club competitions. Some of these changes were driven by the changing nature of football in Europe, some by the developing geopolitical situation in the continent itself and others in response to increased world-wide processes in the elite women's game (UEFA 1998).

Table n°3: National Associations with more than 1,000 registered Under 20 players (1993)

Country	Under 16	Under 20	Total
Belgium	649	1, 053	1, 702
Denmark	13, 000	15, 000	28, 000
England	3, 500	3, 000	6, 500
Finland	5, 344	1, 115	6, 459
France	12, 955	2, 725	15, 680
Germany	25, 000	40, 000	65, 000
Holland	13, 000	5, 000	18, 000
Italy	500	3, 500	4, 000
Norway	30, 000	15, 000	45, 000
Rep. of Ireland	1, 680	720	2, 400
Russia	1, 475	775	2, 250
Spain	290	1, 177	1, 467
Sweden	11, 000	12, 000	23, 000
Switzerland	1, 345	2, 307	3, 652

Source: UEFA 1993 Survey on Girls and Women's Football

4.   Macro Professionalism: Women's Champions' League and Women's World Cups

FIFA Women's World Invitationals, such as the 1984 event in Chinese Taipei, eventually led to the Women's World Championship in 1991. The patronage of women's football consequently increased at the same time that PLC status, the breakaway to form the Premiership and growing global consumption of men's professional leagues became less subject to the control of the national football associations. Equality and diversity has therefore been as much a pragmatic response to the remaining areas under national association control as an ethically-driven impetus. The growing awareness of tournament-football as products to be marketed was another factor in the move towards increased competitions, which have led to increased player segmentation (U20, U17) and more sub-brands. Football competitions, like other sporting mega-events, saw a rise in overall profitability. This, in turn, led to the branding of more products with which to generate both income and a higher awareness of each sport. However these products have very different values. In 2009/10 the UEFA Champions League (for men) paid in 802 million Euros, of which even the smaller clubs knocked out in the early rounds earned a proportion (UEFA 2010/1: 13). Women's club and national team competition received just over 2 million Euros the same year. In 2010/1 season the value of the Champion's League to participating clubs was 830 million Euros; while over the budget distributed to participating women's football teams was cut to just over one million Euros for the same period (UEFA 2010/1: 13). Could the same formula be adapted to promote the commercial and public relations profile of club-football for women in Europe?

The UEFA Women's Champions' League

Increasing youth and club competition for women became a priority of the late 1990s in Europe. UEFA rules for an Under 18 national team tournament were drawn up, and in 1997 Denmark beat France to the inaugural title. Though there had been youth competitions, especially in the Nordic countries, this was another increasingly visible sign of official support for women's football. When this became allied with the male structures of UEFA and became an Under 19 competition in the 2001/2 season Germany continued to win for the third successive year (and again in 2006 and 2007). In 2010 France became the only other European country to have won for a second time (after first winning in 2003), though Sweden (1999); Spain (2004); Russia (2005); Italy (2008) and England (2009) have also taken the title.

A questionnaire to test the viability and interest in European club competition for women, produced positive responses: votes for an official league were strongly for this initiative (No 8, Yes 38); for an official club Cup or an International Club tournament (No 15, Yes 31) and for a Youth Championship (No 16, Yes 30) (UEFA 2001a: 6).

The UEFA Executive Committee approved the proposal to introduce a European Women's club competition in 2000, and thus the UEFA Women's Cup was inaugurated. Frankfurt's Waldstadion provided the venue for the Women's Cup final where a crowd of 12,000 people was described as a record for European women's club football (UEFA 2001b:3). It was the last match to be played at the arena in its 72-year history before its reconstruction in time for Germany to host the 2006 FIFA World Cup finals. Taking part were Umeå IK from Sweden and hosts 1. FFC Frankfurt, who won 2-0 thanks to goals from Steffi Jones and Birgit Prinz. Frankfurt were to win the tournament again in the 2005/6 tournament and again in 2007/8. Umeå IK won twice in successive years 2002/3 and 2003/4. The team was helped to a large extent by the signing of Marta for the second title, where the first leg was played in front of 5,409 spectators and the second 9,500 at the Bornheimer Hang Stadium. Over 420,000 TV viewers in Sweden and 210,000 viewers in Germany watched this second leg in Frankfurt. Arsenal won in 2006/7, and Duisburg in 2008/9. For its ninth season in 2009/10 the competition was re-launched as the UEFA Women's Champions' League. The other title-holder has been 1. FFC Turbine Potsdam in 2004/5 and 2009/10, thus becoming the first winners of the UEFA Women's Champion's League.

This expanded tournament had fifty-three contenders in 2010/1 and the changing nature of European football was reflected in clubs like Zvezda from Russia becoming more prominent. While the expansion of the Women's Champions' League is therefore very encouraging and its profile growing, a seeding system is designed to ensure that the sixteen best teams begin the competition by playing the return leg at home. This, and a rule preventing clubs from the same association being drawn against each other, is designed to simultaneously spread the matches across Europe, but also to ensure rigorous competition (UEFA 2009b: 1-2). The phases played from the thirty-two team round onwards, earn each club 20,000 Euros via its national association, which may, in turn, deduct costs for referees. From the Quarter Finals onwards, only one sponsor is allowed on the front of the shirt and none on the shorts and socks. All other items of clothing and equipment must be free of sponsorship. All other aspects of the competition, from what should be provided to eat and drink, to where the cameras should be positioned and dope testing protocols are stipulated by UEFA (2009a). Earnings were distributed between the finalists, the host association and UEFA. Craven Cottage hosted the 2011 Women's Champions' League Final on 26 May, two nights before the men's UEFA Champions' League Final at Wembley. In 2012, the venue moved to Chelsea.

In this market of scattered and multiple opportunities, individual players remain very much on their own when it comes to their career. Unlike their male counterparts who are supported by the players' unions, such as the Professional Footballers' Association (PFA) in England, and who receive attractive wages, health benefits, advice on how to invest their earnings and so forth, women footballers often lack formal labour rights or adequate health insurance. So, how can female football migrants gain long-lasting social capital and establish viable post-playing careers? There is still plenty of evidence of individual women negotiating their own career pathways. In spite of a reputation that some of its women, such as Sonia Bompastor, are amongst the highest paid in Europe, the women's league in France falls under the control of amateur football. So structural forces sometimes «push» women to play in the United States. Other times we can see «push» and «pull» factors. Ifeoma Dieke, a member of the Scotland women's national team first made her debut in January 2004 against Greece and went on to play in seven qualifying matches for the 2007 FIFA Women's World Cup. Dieke earned her 50th international cap in May 2009, and was honored before Scotland's 3-1 victory over Northern Ireland. However, her skills were developed in the United States, at Florida International University from 1999-2003 before joining the Women's United Soccer Association's Atlanta Beat in 2003. After the suspension of the WUSA franchise she moved to Sweden's Damallsvenskan, appearing for Qbik in 2007 and Kristianstad DFF in 2008. After signing a WPS contract as a free agent Dieke signed as a defender for Boston Breakers in the

2011 Women's Professional Soccer league. Following its suspension, the next transitional phase of her career will be interesting to follow.

There was a strong Swedish presence in the Women's Professional Soccer league rosters for 2010 and 2011 with Kosovare Asllani, Jessica Landström, Madelaine Edlund also making the draft alongside Norway's Solveig Gulbrandsen, Denmark's Johanna Rasmussen, Finland's Laura Kalmari, Holland's Daphne Koster, Switzerland's Ramona Bachmann and France's Sonia Bompastor. While there is a separate legal entity in Sweden, the Elitföreningen Damfotboll (EDF), who have jurisdiction over professional women's football, operate under the umbrella, financially and administratively, of Associations Svenska Fotbollförbundet (SvFF), the Swedish FA. On the one hand, the EDF will continue to benefit from a 1.5 billion kronor-deal with sports media rights agency Kentaro (the equivalent of around £150 million over five years) that is shared between themselves, the SvFF and the Föreningen Svensk Elitfotboll (SEF) from 2011 to 2015. On the other, evidence suggests that Sweden has provided female playing talent for a wide range of semiprofessional leagues across the world and is more likely to export players than import them.

How then, has the Champions' League changed women's soccer? There are many different marketing strategies used by the Champions' League clubs too numerous to develop here but generally the demographics of the «feminist-fathers»; «soccer-moms» and others identified by academic research as supporters of the women's game are under-exploited commercially. As an example, before moving on to the case of the attempt to brand a Women's Super League FCZ Frauen provided two interesting instances of female migration related to women who have moved for careers in football. The first was a marketing executive, Marion Daube, who had not, herself, played the game. She said:

I never played football myself. I studied Business economics with a specialization in Marketing. Then I got involved in my hometown Frankfurt, Germany with women's football and started a project called «girls kick», football fun events for girls. When I moved to Zurich, I started first again as a consultant in a marketing and communications agency, and on a voluntary basis as a marketing consultant in the women's club before I got the opportunity to work full time for the FC Zurich Frauen, which was integrated into the structures of the men's professional club, FC Zurich. Most of our players are Swiss and from the local area. Recently we had one player from Finland. She married a Swiss man and therefore, moved close to Zurich and joined our club. For a few months, we also had a player from New Zealand in our squad. Her mother is Swiss and she came to Switzerland for a while. This was temporary and informal, it was not a permanent move. We do not have a marketing plan and therefore the participation in the UEFA Women's Champions League has not changed. However, we can say that the participation in the UEFA Women's Champions League is a success. Just because of the name and the famous background as well as the uniqueness helps to create more interest with all parties and stakeholders. It is easier to sell the game to sponsors, attract more spectators and use a bigger stadium. It has helped a lot to promote women's football both locally and in our community.

There was perhaps more equivocation in the response I got from from Per Iversen, an executive at Røa, in Norway, regarding the state of professionalism in their team and the wider publicity attendant from the Champions' League:

We do get some inquiries from foreign players, but most of the time these players are not interesting to us, that is, not on the skill level we are looking for/demanding. Presently we have only Norwegian players in our squad. This is the similar to the situation in 2010. As the leading female team in Norway over the last decade, we are drawing attention from potential players from all over Norway. Presently we have several players born and raised well outside the Oslo-region. Most players are students, and therefore Oslo is an interesting area also in that respect. Other reasons than football might lead potential players to Oslo, and Røa. No female footballer is able to make a living solely on football wages... We have approx 20 players in the squad and the total salary budget for 2011 is less US$ 200,000. Participating in the Women's Champions League has not helped us, or the national FA, in terms of getting more publicity, sponsors or general attention towards female football. As far as I know, there has been no changes in marketing plans or anything else as a result of the Women's Champions League - not on Norwegian FA level, or club level.

The Women's Super League: the English model of professionalism 2011

The Football Association took full control of women's football in 1993, having previously supported the Women's Football Association (WFA), somewhat distantly since 1969. In 2002 football overtook netball as the most popular participation sport in England and there are now over 150,000 FA-affiliated players. Between 1998 and 2003 the FA had invested £1.2 million; the National Lottery had granted £8 million and the Football Foundation £2.25 million total for a total spend on girls and women's football of £11.5 million. In addition, £60 million had been put into grassroots football. The additional grants and funding had been leveraged through health, crime, drugs, education, community cohesion and social deprivation projects. Having spoken with Mary Guest; Tessa Hayward; Rachel Pavlou; Kelly Simmons and Zoe Wishman of the FA, it is clear that licensing by the national association is the model for the newly-launched Women's Super League (WSL) of eight teams. At around £3 million spent on the project in 2010/1, the national association was also the major stakeholder. This is the culmination of fourteen years of work as, in 1997, the FA approved the its first Women's Football Talent Development Plan. This levered new funding to establish a network of 50 FA Girls' Centres of Excellence across England licensed by the national association. Having used a series of five-year development plans to lobby for more funding from the governing body, women's football has helped the Corporate Social Responsibility programme of the association, in addition to its equity and diversity agenda, by targeting areas of government concern to draw in external income streams.

English women national team players were also offered central contracts for the first time in the 2008/9 season. Twenty England women's contracts of £16,000 per annum were available, centrally issued by the FA and annually negotiated from 1 December to 30 November each year, paid in monthly installments. The contract covers training requirements, national team image, national fixtures and some promotional rights. A player was entitled to work up to 24 hours a week in another job and hence, rather than being a full-time professional agreement the contracts were seen as providing the «freedom to train». This was because the fitness of so many England players was in need of improvement because of holding down employment and training in what free time was left. Freedom to train is not, however, an entitlement to play or a right to selection. The application process for this was handled by the Professional Footballers' Association as so few women have agents, though the union considers the players semi-professionals. An increase in player salaries to £26,000 was negotiated for 2012/3.

None of American-based England national team players for 2009/10 had central contracts (these included Kelly Smith and Alex Scott at the Boston Breakers; Eniola Aluko at Saint Louis Athletica; Anita Asante and Karen Bardsley at Sky Blue FC or Karen Carney and Katie Chapman at the Chicago Red Stars). However, when the leagues owners suspend operations for the 2011 Women's Professional Soccer season, some players negotiated contracts in the United States as «free agents», while others, like Karen Carney, returned to England. Carney felt that the 2009 move to Chicago was one of the best experiences of her life, as she was young, just out of university, and got to play professional football. There seemed to be a number of factors in Carney's decision to return to Birmingham: these included overcoming injury to be fit for the approaching World Cup, increased opportunities for the national team coach to watch her play regularly and boost selection chances, plus less travelling.

There was a clear message from the English association that returning women players to domestic football is a priority. In order to have a central contract there is a stipulation that a player must be home-based in order for their training to be monitored and so they «must be registered to play for a football club affiliated to an English County FA». I was told that while the application process was open to all, none of the US-based players applied. Paradoxically, earning a living as a player in the US would not be exempt from the 24-hour rule. Controlling both the league and the national team was, however, meant to increase synergy for the English female elite of the game. The motivations for creating the League stem in part from wanting England players to play full time in England, but also to provide a more stable platform for greater competitiveness in the Women's Premier League (which the FA took over in 2004). There had traditionally been problems of over-concentration of the best playing talent in a relatively few teams, such as Arsenal, Fulham and Croyden. On the one hand this meant that results could be predicted before games, and on the other it meant that if a club withdrew suddenly from the league, as Fulham did, then the effects are disproportionate for women's football as a whole. In the wider context of the sport's development, the mainstay of female competition for twenty-plus years was volunteer-created regional leagues and these have been increasingly replaced by 40 FA-initiated county structures. The reconfiguration in 2001/2 meant that any new women's team had to join a county league and remain there until promotion to a regional league. A new four-year strategy will be devised from 2012, with current targets to create an additional 1,281 girls' teams by then. In each of these county leagues there was evidence of movement across regions and the British home nations, but there are also examples, such as Keynsham in Somerset which is next to an international college, where the player mix was more diverse.

The Women's Super League began with eight teams because Hope Powell prioritized the quality of football that is played in a «less is more» strategy. The sixteen clubs who had applied to join were: Arsenal Ladies;

Barnet; Birmingham City Ladies; Bristol Academy Women; Chelsea Ladies; Colchester United Ladies; Doncaster Rovers Belles; Everton Ladies; Leeds Carnegie Ladies; Leicester City; Lincoln Ladies; Liverpool; Millwall Lionesses FC; Newcastle United Women's FC; Nottingham Forest and Sunderland Women, though Leeds later withdrew due to financial problems. The North and North East in particular, are therefore not included and there have been accusations of a southern bias. There are also wider criticisms about the much-vaunted sustainability of the exercise considering that each club had to have a business plan to raise £70,000 a season in the first two years which would be match-funded by the FA. Sunderland, who could guarantee £49,000, were de-selected on this basis. An official from this club and another who prepared Birmingham City's bid (who both asked to remain anonymous) suggested that clubs had inflated their expected spectator figures in the documentation because the FA had communicated their minimum requirements in this regard. Doncaster Belles first game against Lincoln on 13th April 2011 attracted 750 spectators, while the more publicized Arsenal versus Chelsea tie saw 2,200 supporters pay between nothing and £6 a ticket.

Slow and conservative growth were the key messages of the Women's Super League. Each club may pay four players each year in excess of £20,000 (central England contracts are excluded) which was increased in 2012 to £26,000. If any player is earning more than basic expenses, they must have a written contract. Three sources of income are therefore available under the Women's Super League payment scheme: one a central England contract; two, the club contract and three, additional duties, such as administration, ambassadorial work or coaching. Three ambassadorial posts per team are part-funded by the FA, these are subject to the salary cap and the non-playing obligations are part of the contract. A draft system was thought to be good for competitive clubs but unpalatable for players and limiting overseas players would have been also problematic legally. Though a player would need a work permit in order to play if a non-EU citizen, in order to get a work permit a player would have to have to have played a percentage of national team games in the period stipulated by the Home Office and that national team must be in the top 100ish in the world. At the time of writing, no players require work permits to be employed by the league because either EU rules or dual nationality allows them freedom of movement. This and other factors may change. Income and revenue distribution will be reviewed after two years. For example, the FA may allow 40% of club income for wages. The relative balance of FA and commercial interest in the long-term future of the Women's Super League remains to be seen.

How, then, has the Women's Super League been conceptualized as a product and brand? Messages and communications across the FA group now run on a two monthly cycle, focusing on one main product, using television, match-day boards, programmes, YouTube, Facebook and Twitter. So the Superleague really began to be sold in March 2011. Marketing rationale began with the premise that Women's Premier League is not a tangible product to sell, and so there was a need to create a fan-base, mostly comprised of girls aged 9-15. Rather than launch a thirty-six team franchise based on the existing women's Premiership, which would spread the playing talent too far, a Licensing system sought to give coherence to a smaller inaugural group. ESPN, the pay-for-TV broadcaster identified a slot on Tuesdays at 6.30 for a highlights package and also bought rights to production and cross-league footage. In addition to product FAWSL.com each of the eight clubs has a website of similar standard, design, product and branding perspective.

Gender was downplayed as part of the media story and the «new» product emphasis has been on a summer league as a differentiating factor. This has been perceived within the FA as news for the media, in a quiet time for football, although the first game was played 13th April 2011, a busy time in the fixture list in domestic leagues and international competitions. A break was scheduled after the teams' seventh match on 12th May 2011, so games resumed in late July and completed in August. This means that the WSL launched somewhat awkwardly around the scheduling for Women's World Cup in Germany.

Sustainability has been the key message of the WSL but the lack of national coverage, with two Liverpool and two London teams, and interruptions to the media presentation have challenged this. Telling a coherent public relations story about women's football and making players accessible were other aspects of the Unique Selling Point. This was not so very different from the way that WUSA or WPS was conceptualized. Female players were very connected to their audience and accessible. The WSL live experience was also intended to borrow from the grass-roots marketing that proved such a successful ticket sales strategy in WWC '99. The WSL was conceived to be family-orientated, match-day kits comprised photo boards, cameras, laptops to look at Facebook and live entertainment at each of the clubs. Since 9-15 year old girls were the primary target market teen media such as Shout and Bliss have also been prioritised. Celebrity endorsements included Parade, a girl band at the launch match. N-Dubz, a hip-hop band originally from Camden, had a female vocalist Tulisa Contostavlos who was known to enjoy football and she was approached to act as an ambassador. Instead she undertook a more lucrative deal to appear as a judge on the televised singing talent show The X Factor. Branding the stadiums to have uniform appearance was also key in presenting the league to a media audience. The FA wanted four commercial partners and had two in their first season: a financial services provider, Yorkshire Building Society and Continental Tyres, a multinational car tyre manufacturer.

Pre-launch focus groups, with female football players aged 9-15, suggested avoiding an image that was too girly, fluffy, or pink as this would discredit what they felt to be a serious enthusiasm. Clichés such as «On the ball with the beautiful game – here come the girls» still appeared during the Women's World Cup in Germany. For the most part these formulaic narratives have been avoided: the colours purple and grey were instead felt to be neutral but a dynamic backdrop for each club's own colours. Rather than a female player, a somewhat amorphous image of a football and a small star made up the logo along with the letters The FA WSL.

Digital ambient marketing included the use social-networking habits and technologies in an interactive format entitled *Call the Shots*. An interactive generation was asked what music should be played at half time when a goal was scored, what should the league mascot be called and so on. Players were educated in merchandising awareness and expected to take part in marketing the club and league brand. No alcohol, gambling or cosmetics endorsements were agreed. Nor was an overtly sexualized glamour been used in photo-shoots compared with recent FIFA promotional campaigns using models like Adriana Sklenarikova, wife of Christian Karembeu, even though she had never played the game. Women's football was instead being «normalised» through its multiple femininities as an aspirational, athletic, attractive, fun, approachable version of the game. This was extended to media training for players in how to handle the negative stereotypes that, while diminishing, continued to surround female participants.

In spite of claims for professional aspects of women's football made here, a considerable caveat remains that the thirty-member European Professional Football Leagues (EPFL), which was founded in 2005, has no female leagues affiliated. It has no immediate plans to incorporate women's leagues within its scope of activities despite core values promoting Unity, Professionalism and Reformism. This is largely due to questions over sustainability, effective commercialization rights and player union structures in the current formulations of women's football. There is evidently some way to go before «a right to train» becomes full professionalism in a commercially vibrant league. However there are cautious plans to expand the league after its second season, so this may have been a wise strategy. The BBC has also expressed more of an interest in women's football since the success of the 2012 Olympics so public broadcasting might provide new forms of media support.

5.   Conclusion: From FIFA Women's World Cup Germany 2011 to Canada 2015

On 29 October 2010 the FIFA Executive Committee approved an increase in the prize money to be awarded at the 2011 FIFA Women's World Cup of US$ 1.2 million; bringing the total available to US$ 7.6 million (FIFA Exco Summary 2010: 15). The Women's World Cup remained the most lucrative showcase of elite female football talent at the time of writing, far surpassing that of any domestic league or club-based competition. The FIFA WWC Germany 2011 budget extended to 51 million Euros, most of which was to be recouped by ticket sales: this was a challenging prospect, even in a country which sought to be the first to win a third consecutive World Cup. More than 400,000 tickets sold earlier than expected. Germany won the FIFA Women's World Cups in 2003 and 2007 respectively but revenues were lost when they were defeated by the eventual title winners, Japan, in the 2011 quarter finals. The USA remains the other dominant force in the tournament, winning the inaugural title in PR China 1991 and on home soil in 1999, in front of a crowd of 93,000 spectators. FIFA launched an Under 19 Women's World Championship hosted by Canada in 2002 which the US also won. From 2008 this was re-named a World Cup and aligned with male competitions to become an Under 20 event, again won by the US in Chile that year. Germany won in 2004 and 2010 while North Korea took the title in the 2006 edition, hosted by Russia.

The United States remain the only team to have reached the semi-final of each Women's World Cup to date, though Norway was also an important contender, having lost in the final in 1991 and winning a twelve-team tournament in 1995. Of late, Brazil has become a significant team, reaching third in 1999, losing the final in 2007 and providing key individuals in the women's game. Canada has finished in fourth place in 1999 and Sweden had a third place in 1991 and lost the final in 2003. Brazil, PR China, Germany, Japan, Nigeria, Norway, Sweden and USA are the only countries that have been part of all five previous editions of the Women's World Cup. While sufficiently established to have its own set of traditions and statistics such as those above, there remains a problem of how to pitch the competition to the media, more especially when it expands to a twenty-four team tournament in 2015 in Canada. What can we conclude from the place of the World Cup in professionalizing football as an occupation for women?

In her survey of women's changing place in Europe over 300 years Simonton describes a gradual move from what she calls «intimate spaces» of self, home and family to wider community roles including friendships to elected office and then shaping wider national and international cultures (2011: 389). This pattern of shift can be seen in a compressed form for women's place in football between 1971 and 2011 in terms of playing, coaching and administration. While this project has tried to identify these main shifts, it is also about the continuities that predominate in the twenty-first century as football shows itself to be more conservative than even the International Olympic Committee (IOC) in preparing to have its first elected woman onto the FIFA Executive Committee. We know that women have been participating in football since the early 1880s at least and yet the number of women who can earn a living wage from the game remains, at best, a hundred or so worldwide. By comparison Olympic sports, which first saw female participation in 1900 and were amateur until 1984, can offer financially lucrative careers to at least some of the 5,000 female participants expected in 2012.

The Women's World Cup particularly, and international competition generally, have undoubtedly been a major motor for the professionalization of women's football in terms of providing a platform for elite specialization, a product to be sold to sponsors and spectators alike plus an increasing calendar of fixtures. In PR China in 1991 just 45 national teams competed in the first worldwide qualifying round and there were fewer than 100 women's international matches played a year (Kunz 2010: 44-5). For Germany 2011 a record 122 national teams competed in 355 qualifying matches for that competition alone. In 2010 women's international matches numbered 512, played by 141 countries. However, of FIFA's 208 member associations 185 men's representative teams played that year, compared with 141 women's squads. A long-term aim to include more national associations to develop, promote and support women's football remains a priority therefore. It should also be noted that the quadrennial cycle of the Women's World Cup Finals sees peaks and troughs in this overall rising trend. In spite of 368 internationals between 100 women's national teams in 2003, just 255 matches between 84 countries took place in 2005. Similarly, 447 fixtures in 2006 between 134 women's national teams fell to 307 international matches between 86 countries in 2009 (Kunz 2010: 44-5).

One tension in the current formulations of women's semi-professional leagues is between national association intervention and market forces. At the moment national associations have taken it upon themselves to encourage and assist existing women's clubs and to mould new leagues, rather than opening the women's game to the market. An aspect of the problems can be shown by the English Women's Super League club Birmingham City, who had thought to use the Women's FA Cup as a way of raising their profile in the game more generally and, in particular their financial income. However, in spite of intensive pre-season preparation for the Super League, they lost their FA cup match in March 2011 to Barnet, a team based in the current Women's Premiership, not in the elite eight. This was attributed to a change in the playing season for the WSL in its April to August schedule, while those women who were used to the traditional calendar for football were more match-fit. There may be something to this, but it had followed a month-long training camp by the England team in Cyprus the previous month, so it is not entirely convincing as an explanation. Unlike the German Women's Bundesliga, many of the Super League teams have dropped their reserve sides to concentrate on their squad of twenty and so the depth of the playing personnel outside the eight teams is also an issue for analysis. In any case, the broader question is whether licensing and benchmarking will translate to an overall increase in playing standards, and furthermore, if that will increase national squad performances in more European countries.

There are though promising developments in terms of European-wide awareness over the need both to develop the mass of participants and elite players, as the recent KISS development workshop held by UEFA on the 24-25th February 2011 in Nyon, indicated. The Women's Football Development Programme (WFDP) has made 100,000 Euros per year per national association available, incentivized for administrative and playing development. This is supplemented by KISS workshops and expert advice in a working group drawn mainly from the Women's Committee, notably Karen Espelund (Norway); Susanne Erlandsson (Sweden); Vera Pauw (technical director for the Russia FA women's team); Sheila Begbie (Scotland) and Aleksandra Nikolovska (FYR Macedonia). Tools like the Gender Empowerment Index (GEM) are also allowing comparison of the number of female football players with the percentage of women in a total population. This leads to more sophisticated sports development, and grouping together countries for relevant development. Women are now being more thoroughly integrated into marketing campaigns, such as the Star Challenge *Woody and Wulfy in Bilbao* (UEFA 2007b). So, as the concluding chapter outlines, there are complexities around understanding the many kinds of professionalisms for women in football and its many cultural transfers.

Conclusion: Mobility, Professionalism and Football's Changing Cultural Values

> *Sport remains one of the most conservative and inflexible areas of public life, lagging far behind other social structures. Distributional data has demonstrated that in Europe, despite more than a decade of strategies and actions to support progress towards gender equity in sports organisations, women are still under-represented in executive and decision-making positions (Talbot 2000).*

When Fanny Blankers-Koen won four gold medals at the 1948 London Olympic Games as a thirty year old mother of two, the British Press called her «The Flying Housewife». In 2011, Emma Byrne, the Arsenal Ladies' Irish goalkeeper was also praised for her domestic skills, after telling a magazine that after football, she enjoyed making bread (Sky Sports 2011: 17). That a magazine like Sky Sports should feature a woman footballer at all indicates how much has changed in the last sixty years. Foregrounding her domestic abilities as the focus of the article illustrates continuities in the cultural value of sport and in media perceptions of female of athletes. Football's «manly» customs have been enduring, even while research into female participation over the last century is now well-established in academic circles and cultural industries (Yates and Vasilli 2011). Several young adult fiction titles dedicated to themes around women's soccer which also draw on longer histories dating back to The Football Favourite in the early 1920s (Bhattacharya 1992; Boaler 1994; Dhami 2011; Pielichaty 2009). So it is important to emphasise that both on the pitch and off, the meanings around the game have long been contested.

In the search to give a feminine-appropriate image to women's football, one approach has been to emphasise a very girly, youthful «pink» image to the game. As an example, Sue Ronan of the FA of Ireland credits the Soccer Sisters campaign aimed at 7-12 year girls, including an Aviva-sponsored pink kit and cerise water bottle, with doubling participation numbers to 21,590 at that age (2011). As has been seen by the example of the Women's Super League, in some cases this use of pink has been seen as trivialising female participation and, as such, purple has been used in branding a more empowered, mature dynamic for the brand. It may seem a rather trivial and distracting point to highlight the use of a particular colour in imagining and branding football as a female-appropriate sport but it is clear that pink is, like the use of the phrase «beautiful game», now a cliché in trying to normalise the participation of women and girls. With a tag line «The Beautiful Side of 20Eleven» the Women's World Cup in Germany has trademarked the phrase as integral to the presentation of the woman player. A Siobhan Tarr mosaic called The Pink Side (2011) was be exhibited at the Schwules (Gay) Museum Berlin during the Women's World Cup 2011 along with nineteen other commissions by contemporary artists June to August 2011 as part of the cultural celebrations of that event (Schwules Museum 2011). These representations evidence that football has plenty of founding mothers, daughters, sisters, aunts and mentors in its history and heritage, as well as the more well-known fathers, sons, brothers and uncles. In a world where the humanities is increasingly squeezed in favour of hard sciences, business, law and technology, funding a history project in the first tranche of the UEFA Research Grant Programme may remind us that, in our enthusiasm for the present and future prospects of women's football, we should not forget the past.

The earliest examples of women's football in the nineteenth century sought to draw a paying audience to see female competition. Commodification was a part of the early processes. Individual presentation, as with other expressions of personal identity, negotiated a path between what was commercially available and what they felt was respectable. If the migration of the players in these early leagues might better be understood as transitory movement, personal networks were nevertheless significant. This included both how to play football under codified rules and how to improve performance. Most of the early twentieth century teams were formed either by workers of the same factory, such as the most famous British example, the Dick, Kerr Ladies of Lancashire or, as the case of Fémina, by diversifying from gymnastics. Fémina toured England in March 1920, first playing Dick, Kerr's in Preston. The image of the kiss of welcome between the two captains to open the first match was widely circulated across Europe: from this moment on mediated international matches and regional competition were an important part of the story of women's football.

Female football migration was very evident in this early period. Competitive rivalry extended by 1921 to one hundred and fifty British teams including Liverpool, Birmingham, Bath and Plymouth and «internationals» against Scottish, French and Belgian women's teams. A planned US and Canada Dick, Kerr's tour, a form of which eventually took place in late 1922, saw them play against male professionals with Lily Parr as captain and the «star draw». Parr is thought to have earned 10 shillings a game for her entire playing career, until she retired in 1951. Alice Mills, who had never previously been out of Britain before this tour followed many other Lancashire cotton migrants and moved to the Pawtucket area the following year, retiring from football to raise a large family and remaining in the United States for the rest of her life. If some of the «pull» factors at this time were the opportunity to play football at the highest level, the «push» factors could include wider economic forces. Nevertheless, the principle of «signing on» the best player (s) of the opposing team was established at the outset. So the timeframe of this current project could be extended to incorporate this earlier period in future research.

By 1921, the English Football Association had banned women from the fields of Football League and Association clubs in England, in part because players «expenses» absorbed too much from charity money raised and because it was «unsuitable». If male professional players were to be controlled by maximum wage caps and the retain and transfer system, however difficult these were to police, female professionalism was not to be tolerated. As has been seen, this antipathy towards women's football generally permeated most of Europe but did not always lead to an outright embargo. Women in France began playing at a similar time to those in Britain and promoted the popularity of the sport internationally in part via the Women's Olympic Games from 1921, which were retitled Women's World Games between 1926 and 1934. These were pioneered Alice Milliat in protest at female exclusion from many disciplines at the Olympic Games (revived in its modern form by Baron De Coubertin as a festival intended for male youth). A 1923 game in Barcelona, between a French and an English team, remains among the earliest important examples of player migration when Florrie Redford (formerly a prolific striker of Dick, Kerr's) seems to have played for Les Sportives (Williams 2003: 45). Women's football also developed in Germany and Austria after the First World War and there seems to be evidence of a game in Russia (of which we know little) in 1911.

Women's sport more broadly, represents an area of scant historical inquiry compared to other facets of life in Europe such as religion, politics, family, education, work, and community institutions. Nevertheless, European women's football has a history going back to the nineteenth century and intersects with each of the areas listed above. This female tradition is often overlooked in favour of a story of rejection of women players by the sport's governing bodies and the cultural implications of that attitude, which ranged across the continent from prohibition to antipathy. In the current era of overt progressivism, this long-standing agency on behalf of women players could be more often and explicitly told as part of football's history because it shows the extent of the game's universal appeal for over a century. Not least, Roland Robertson has defined globalisation as a concept that «refers both to the compression of the world and the intensification of consciousness of the world as a whole» (1992:8). While this work has traced greater connectivity (more migration and digital communication) and globality (people reflecting on the state of the world and their place in it) were evident in Europe during the period 1971-2011 in women's football, we can also see traces of these processes in earlier phases of popularity.

As the Introduction of this work has shown, cultural, social, economic and political changes spread across Europe after 1945 and there was an increase of women participating in sport, including football, giving rise to what can appear to be the late modernity of women's football. Events in Europe included the formation of a West German Women's Football Association in Essen in August 1955 with twenty-two clubs. Who were these players and what can this period tell us about women's football at the time? This was followed by the 2-1 victory in an international with the Netherlands in 1956 in front of a crowd of 18,000 in Essen and then, in 1957 to a European Women's Championship with the final in the 40,000-seater Poststadium a 4-1 victory for «England» over «West Germany». However, in the Pathé newsreel footage of this tournament nothing is made of the humiliation of English football in 1953 by Hungary or Germany's 1954 success in the World Cup and so it seems to stand apart from those defining «football» moments. What we need to ask in reviewing these early periods therefore are questions like: How significant was the 1954 World Cup victory for German women's football? What did the audience in the cinema make of these newsreels as sport, entertainment, and mediated public spectacle in Germany, in England and across Europe? FIFA, by its own admission only began researching early women's football matches during the last few years and claims of the «first» official international between France and the Netherlands in April 1971 is open to debate (Duret 2011: 34-9).

After initially modifying the rules to make them less «rough» for women in the 1960s, the DFB then abandoned the modifications and gave official permission for women's matches to be played as double headers prior to men's professional matches. So by May 1970 at an FC Kaiserslautern versus FC Cologne match, the Landau and Augsburg women's teams played in front of 18,000 people. Matches in the 1950s, 1960s and 1970s were often played as part of a town's Volkfest, annual people's fair, and filled town stadiums. In 1990 the formation of a regional North East league consisted of teams from the GDR. Berlin hosted the formation of a National League North and South with most clubs being sections of local sports clubs and football one of a number of sports played. Some of the key teams in German women's football have been TuS Worrstadt (formed in 1969) who won the first national championship in 1974 and Bergish Gladbach (formed in 1973) who won the national championship 1977 and also the Cup Final in 1981, 1982 and 1984. Bayern Munich, who won the national championship in 1976, were runners up in 1979 and also runners up in their Cup Final appearances in 1988 and 1990.

Before the reunification of Germany in 1990, 1. FFC Turbine Potsdam (fully known as «1. Frauen-Fußball-Club Turbine Potsdam 71 e. V») dominated the East German women's league. It remains the only club from the former East Germany to win the unified title. The team also won the UEFA women's competition in the 2004/5 season, beating the Swedish team of Djurgården/Älvsjö 5-1 overall in the final. Turbine Potsdam have been the most significant East German team to maintain a place in the Frauen Bundesliga, after integration and the national team benefited a great deal from East German players, in spite of the fact that the women had not been supported at all by the East German Football Association because it was not considered to be a top-level (Olympic) sport. In contrast, male players had been treated favourably by both the ruling party and the state in spite of unfavourable cost-benefit ratios in terms of their international achievements. If there was variation within Germany, development across the major countries of Europe was considerably more uneven. The football association of Denmark, for example, incorporated women's football in 1972 despite clubs such as BK Femina being formed in 1959. This gradual acceptance created some player fluxes to particular centres of football at particular times. As the national associations reversed their previous institutional discouragement to include the growing participation of women into officially-sanctioned football leagues, the concentrations of players across clubs changed. These leagues have produced a network of proto-professionalism enabling women to begin to negotiate paid work by migrating to play football. Much work on this period remains to be done.

The Frauen Bundesliga has been of considerable importance to women's football generally as it is estimated that since 2000 the DFB has invested over 100 million Euros in the development of Germany's young football talent. This is encouraging, as Cup Finals have been played in Berlin prior to the Men's matches since 1985 and women's teams have been paid 13,000 to 21,000 Euros a year, including TV money, of which the DFB decides the proportion. However, the Frauen Bundesliga has an importance beyond Germany itself because it provides elite competition and some employment for players from national teams who have yet to break through into World Cup competition. This can be seen in the case of quite wealthy countries, such as Switzerland, where domestic playing opportunities are limited. Marisa Brunner, Martina Moser and Danique Stein played for German clubs in 2009/10.

A gradual but widening public recognition of women who pioneered professional and semi-professional roles in football has become evident. More recently, the increasingly European-wide practice of electing key individuals to respective Halls of Fame has helped. At the National Football Museum, Preston, England Female inductees are Debbie Bampton; Pauline Cope; Gillian Coultard; Sue Lopez; Lily Parr; Hope Powell; Brenda Sempare; Marieanne Spacey; Karen Walker and Joan Whalley have been honoured (2011). Players must be at least thirty years of age and have played for England for five years to qualify. At the Scottish Football Museum Rose Reilly was inducted in 2007. She remains the sole woman to be recognized in this way. Others, like Welsh international Karen Jones have been awarded honours, in this case the Member of the Order of the British Empire (MBE) for services to football as an administrator and volunteer. With more time, it would surely be possible to compile a more comprehensive list of the growing number of women across generations who have been recognized for their contributions to the sport and to society more widely.

To provide a wider context, the football industry as a whole underwent a revolution while women's football took a slower evolution: in spite of considerable national, regional and local variation across Europe in 2011, it is possible to say that across 30 leagues the trans-nationalism of male player movement has increased, with the percentage of expatriates at levels of up to 35% in some clubs in recent years (Poli et al. 2011: 45). However, it is also indicative of how concentrated that market for labour is, when this statistic is balanced by figures which show that the majority of first team players are expatriates in five of thirty-six European leagues. The economic and sporting gaps between championships in European football are consequently subject to considerable variation. Even so, it is possible to say that Western European expatriates are most represented in top leagues, whilst Eastern Europeans are most numerous in the bottom leagues, generally situated in this part of the continent, though the variations are relatively small (Besson et al. 2011: 46-7). Is this also the case for women players?

The varied nature of semi-professionalism makes this difficult to quantify or to definitively state that the individual moved for football-related employment: work permits are still relatively rare and within the EU are not required at all. The only significant case to come before the Court of Arbitration for Sport (CAS), which was recognised in 2002 by FIFA in a move to formalize dispute resolution, has been the case of women moving from Olympique Lyonnais vs UEFA and Fortuna Hjørring in January 2010. CAS cancelled the decision in UEFA's appeal court that gave Fortuna a victory in their protest against Olympique Lyonnais' use of two Norwegian players who they claimed infringed amateur and club transfer rules. It effectively meant that the Women's Champion's League could not be enforced as an amateur competition. In comparison, men's football accounted for one third of the CAS caseload in the same year. Women's football simply has not been legislated and dissected to the degree of the more socio-economic and commercially developed male sector, but this may well change in the next decade.

Some of the case studies and individuals cited here indicate, though, that an emerging market within Europe has provided both alternative and additional opportunities to earn a living from the game compared with those in the United States and the Japanese «L» League. While moving alone for rational reasons including competitive factors, recognition and monetary rewards is central to player motivation, it is relatively rare that players move in isolation. While some in a particular tranche may stay in a particular country longer than others, the networks of participation are often reflected in patterns of movement. This is not so much a process of «pull» and «push» as «drag», since a small group of trialists will often move temporarily together and some will be more successful, and stay for longer than others. The cross-cultural transfer of knowledge and player talent is therefore rarely straightforward. Success is not always measured in football terms; as lifestyle and lifecycle considerations also shape player migration. The new professionalism therefore still owes much to the voluntary and amateur structures that primarily continue to define women's football. Because elite players pool in a relatively few high-profile clubs, they can tend to migrate in small groups to see what the career opportunities in a particular locale are. Significant «pull» factors are the enjoyment of physical labour; social prestige; a pleasant climate; lifestyle and education (from learning new languages to developing academic and vocational skills). Football culture, as expressed in a particular locale, has also been a key driver.

One way of developing this work is to stress an even more diverse range of local responses to purported globalization processes in football. There are many glocalised structures across the European countries to suggest that the sport is best understood by the interplay of global and local forces. For example, this work has established that globally women and girls are an under-developed and readily identifiable sector of the football participant demographic. If there is one consensus that unites those who work in the sector it is that the general profile of the women's game needs to be raised: I have not spoken to one individual who felt that women's football was over-exposed in its public relations profile or over-exploited as a commercial prospect. Why is there not more political will to invest significantly in marketing and sales departments to further strengthen the market share of the women's game?

As a regional response, the new UEFA scheme HatTrick III represents a continuing investment in female football markets at national association level. There is little chance that female European participation will reach levels in which that demographic is fully exploited at any time in the near future. From 2012 to 2016, for example, each UEFA national association will receive €3 million (UEFA EXCO 2010). This is in addition to a further €1.5 million per year, over the four-year period, in solidarity payments that will be linked to commitments such as the implementation of a Club Licensing scheme, participation in competitions and membership of the UEFA Coaching Convention and Grassroots Charter, among others. Therefore, the total amount payable per national association via HatTrick

III is €9 million, which represents an increase of more than 15% in comparison to HatTrick II. In particular, the Executive Committee noted the huge growth in European women's football, both in terms of registered players and participation, and agreed to support the UEFA Women's Football Development Programme (WFDP) via a yearly payment of €100,000 per year between 2012 and 2016, from the HatTrick III payments. While this is encouraging, by definition it limits female development to a relatively small percentage of the overall budget. An interesting, and provocative, proposition might be to require that national associations spend the money equally, 50% each for male and female development.

As individuals and perceived gatekeepers to familial interest, it makes sound business sense to develop female consumers of the game as well as fulfilling sports development and Corporate Social Responsibility agendas (Levermore 2010 221-34). However, the development issues in Norway are unlike those in Germany and different again than priorities in Iceland. As well as being subject to national association structures, the profile of the women's game in each country is subject to considerable regional variation, with accusations that the Women's Super League in England, for example, is too London-centric. This mirrors perceptions since the Football Association took over the women's game in 1993 that a specifically London-dominated national squad selection-process has been in place. The migratory trends highlighted in 2011 therefore look likely to increase as more opportunities present themselves to a growing number of women in European football. The meeting between local conditions, regional priorities and global structures nevertheless shapes that overall rise.

The new markets and key regions for football development include the Middle East, Asia more generally and Africa. For example the German Foreign Office recently organised an eight-team tournament in Bahrain to promote the FIFA Women's World Cup 2011 and women's football in general as part of its outreach activities in non-qualified countries. This is not an isolated initiative. Since 2008, for instance, more than 30 FIFA courses related to women's football have taken place in the Middle East in Iran, Jordan, Kuwait, Lebanon, Palestine, Qatar, Syria, and the United Arab Emirates from beach football, to development seminars, futsal tournaments and refereeing courses (Cox 2011: 32-7). Sheikha Hussa Bint Khalid Abdulla Al Khalifa, at twenty-five years of age, is the first ever female Executive Committee member of the Union of Arab Football Associations.

The individual and group patterns of women football players also reflect some wider trends in migration studies themselves such as the flows and fluxes of skilled and technically-talented females in the workforce, more generally. This project has reflected that players were free to innovate and adapt personal skills to local circumstances. There may be wider trends, such as the educational migrant who stays for a limited span of time to develop or prolong a playing career by one of a number of ancillary occupations, most notably coaching. Others might sustain themselves, a partner or family in their country of occupation or of origin. It is possible to say that making a living as a football player is now no longer the exclusive preserve of men, but that few European women do manage to earn a living entirely from playing at the highest level.

We might judge the development of professionalization by the growing number of women who chose to take up a job in football as athletes, as managers and coaches or in ancillary occupations listed above. What is more problematic, as the case studies have shown, is the move towards a viable post-playing career. While the survey of the Women's Champions' League Clubs and those playing in some of Europe's female elite competitions indicates an increasingly market-oriented attitude towards commercial development, this again is largely dependent upon the voluntary and community structures that have historically been the mainstay. Helping these clubs to conceive of their product as something marketable and with a viable commercial future remains challenging.

As it becomes more normalized to see women professional players as aspirational figures, it may well be that increasing numbers of young girls seek to specialize in football at an increasingly early age. The academic literature around the efficacy of role models on motivating the young is, however sparse, and this is another area that could be studied by longitudinal methods. What we can say, is that to gain recognition and material wealth in football for the foreseeable future, most European women will have to move countries. While some move towards market-driven rationality is detectable, this is an as yet emerging sub-discipline of the football industry. Obvious cultural and geographical factors, such as proximity of migration between countries of origin and destination which are closely linked by language or border are also evident in that the Irish and Welsh may move to England and migration between Scandinavian and Nordic countries also marked. However, another major factor is the distinct shape of European women's football up to the present day. Consequently, female players' movement is often different than male players generally and elite migrants particularly, because of the human geography of club location. While world cities such as London, Paris, Berlin and Copenhagen are part of this story, Lincoln in England, Montpellier in France, Duisburg in Germany and Fortuna Hjorring in Denmark are also part of the map of elite European women's football. So there is no neat fit for the continent's capitals or «world cities» to which fans of the game would normally pay pilgrimage.

Denmark, France, Norway and Sweden provide attractive conditions for migrant women football players, while the Netherlands, Germany and England have proto-professional leagues. Eastern European countries have yet to create elite leagues which draw in significant diasporas of north, west or southern female talent but, as the case of Vera Pauw indicates, there are signs of increasing integration. Whatever the civil processes at work here, the emerging models of European professional women's soccer offer interesting examples of leagues that combine aspects of North American franchises with the traditional models of football. As such, they have wider implications for how the sport is presented to a European and world-wide audience. The English Women's Super League can be seen as perhaps the most Amercanised example of a professional football league in Europe.

What is the future of professional leagues licensed by national associations in Europe? The project has begun to answer some of this question. Trademarks, logos and mascots have been developed; players are increasingly media-trained and aware of community-based public relations opportunities; the media and print journalism has been targeted; digital social networking is key; shirt sponsorship and field boards, tickets, promotional rights for merchandise agreed. The Unique Selling Point appears to be that the players are approachable, modest and accessible workingwomen who love their football and are grateful to be able to play professionally. They are linked with, and give back to their communities. The overwhelming feeling is that female professionalism is multicultural; passionate; humble; community-engaged; diverse and digitally-aware. Within female football's European elite, the leagues' brands combined speak of an inclusive culture around an exclusively talented pinnacle of players.

Europe has been central to the world-wide development of women's football but to what extent will it remain a core of activity that attracts players, rather than being a donor of female talent? The FIFA Executive

Committee in 2005 ratified Russia 2006 as a U20 not U19 competition. They also confirmed the number of slots per delegation for Women's World Cup 2007 as hosts 1, AFC 2, CAF 2, CONCACAF 2.5, CONMEBOL 2, OFC 1 and UEFA 5. An expanded tournament will pressurize European countries to earn a place in a more competitive environment. However, the development of the sport is not isolated to football-only tournaments.

The 2004 Olympic football competition in Athens was the first time that a women's event had been staged as part of a Summer Games in Europe. Three European countries, including hosts Greece, were among the ten in the tournament. Germany and Sweden joined Australia, Brazil, China PR, Japan, Mexico, Nigeria, and the USA (compared with 16 men's teams at the same games). London 2012 provided another increased opportunity to raise the profile of this sport as against others. Questions remain for future research however: Will one of the European examples here become the world's best female soccer league and thereby the new brand for women's football? Should resources be pooled to establish a continent-wide female football league for a new Europe? How will football compare with other professional leagues in other team sports, such as netball, and with individual disciplines where lucrative careers can be made?

Tensions that have been explored here include the strategic philanthropy of the FA owning and promoting a licensed closed Women's Super League, with its limited salary cap. Will this and its counterparts in Germany and the Netherlands retain the best European players? The uncertain market for women's football as a whole is one complicating factor here. The growing trans-national opportunities for female playing-talent are still more. Will the «Atlantic drift» continue in both directions? What will be the long term future of the National Women's Soccer League in the United States? Will other European leagues draw the elite? Notably, Karen Carney has returned from the US to play for Birmingham City in England in 2011. Meanwhile, Gemma Davison (Barnet, England) and Caroline Seger (a Swedish international who had played for Linkopings FC since 2005) and signed for Western New York Flash, for example had to seek alternative employment when WPS suspended operations due to financial problems. Czech international, Vendula Strnadova, who studies in the United States and lived in New Mexico, did not get to play for the Atlanta Beat. Ifeoma Dieke, a member of the Scotland Women's National Team, had to find alternative employment from the Boston Breakers as did England internationals Alex Scott and Kelly Smith. Veronica Boquete and Laura del Rio Garcia of Spain; Holmfridur Magnusdottir of Iceland and Lianne Sanderson of England did not get to play for the Philadelphia Independence. English national team players, Eniola Aluko Anita Asante and Karen Bardsley were forced to leave the squad of Sky Blue FC, based in New Jersey, as did Finland's most capped still-active player Laura Kalmari and Sweden's Therese Sjögran. Evidently, the move to the United States with the college infrastructure, WPS and W leagues, high female participation rates and the prospect of Puma sponsorship and Nike endorsements remains an appealing draw compared with, say, an English WSL sponsored by Continental Tyres and the Yorkshire Building Society. But enforced termination of employment might also lead to a complete change of lifestyle in another country.

To return to a theme first raised in the Introduction of this work, can women's football in Europe develop a sense of «Unity in Diversity»? This implies an inclusiveness of the various stage of development across national associations but also a diverse sense of female identity that the sport can promote including ethnic and religious backgrounds, sexuality, disability, age and class. What is also evident is that international competition will continue to dominate club loyalties for the foreseeable future, in providing an international stage for elite talent. This work then has highlighted that national squad players are but a small percentage of the mobile female football talent in Europe. Future projects could explore as to whether the youth competitions that have been a main growth area in driving overall standards of play up, have encouraged girls and young women to specialize increasingly early in a football-career. Other research and analysis of club operations could identify where business practices differ from volunteer and community initiatives, and where there are areas of overlap.

Appendix 1: Some Key Dates of European Union, integration and expansion[3]

1945 End of World War II

1946 Civil war breaks out in Greece; European Union of Federalists (EUF) formed

1947 Soviet walkout of Four Power Council of Foreign Ministers signals the beginnings of the cold war; Committee for European Economic Co-operation (CEEC) set up

1948 Benelux states (Belgium, the Netherlands and Luxembourg) commence economic union and a European Congress is held at The Hague

1949 Federal Republic of Germany established; North Atlantic Treaty signed in Washington to create NATO and Council of Europe formed

1950 Korean War begins; European Defence Community (EDC) launched and Council of Europe adopts a European Convention on Human Rights

1951 Treaty of Paris establishes the European Coal and Steel Community (ECSC)

1952 European Defence Community Treaty signed in Paris

1953 Draft Treaty for a European Political Community is adopted

1956 USSR invades Hungary to put down an anti-communist rising; France becomes involved in conflict in Algeria and the nationalization of the Suez canal by Egypt resulted in a failed attempt to occupy the zone by France and England

---

3 Compiled from Stephen George and Ian Bache (2001).

1957 The Treaty of Rome establishes the European Economic Community (EEC) and the European Atomic Energy Community (Euratom)

1961 Association Agreement signed with Greece; Britain, Denmark and
Ireland apply for membership

1962 Norway applies to join the EEC

1963 De Gaulle announces his veto of British Membership

1965 The «empty chair crisis» when the French boycotted all Council
of Ministers meetings in protest at how the revenue to finance the
budget would be raised

1966 «Luxembourg compromise» established the principle of national
contributions and national governments would retain the right to
veto

1967 Britain, Denmark, Norway and Ireland make a second application
for membership of the EC; Sweden applies to join; Jean Rey becomes first Commission President for the combined communities
(ECSC, EEC, Euratom)

1968 Merger Treaty comes into effect establishing a Customs Union and
common external tariff

1969 Resignation of President De Gaulle; new German government under chancellor Willy Brandt and his policy of Ostpolitik to improve
relations with the communist bloc; The Hague summit sees 'the
Relaunching of Europe' and commits to completion, widening and
deepening of European integration

1970 Membership negotiations begin with Britain, Ireland, Denmark and
Norway

1971 Collapse of the international monetary system

1972 Start of the «snake in the tunnel» system of EC monetary co-ordination for approximating exchange rates of member currencies while holding their values jointly against the United States dollar

1973 First enlargement of the EC from six to nine member states with the accession of Britain, Denmark and Ireland; the «snake» is broken as the British and Italian governments are forced to float currencies on the international markets; OPEC oil crisis and resultant «stagflation» produces economic divergence in the EC

1974 Turkish invasion of Cyprus; creation of a European Council

1975 Greek application for membership of EC

1977 Roy Jenkins become President of the European Commission and calls for monetary union; Portugese and Spanish applications for membership

1978 Brussels European Council agrees to a European Monetary System (EMS)

1979 First direct elections to the European Parliament; Margaret Thatcher demands a British budget rebate

1981 Greece becomes the tenth member of the EC

1985 Portuguese and Spanish accession treaties signed to join the following year as the EC expands to twelve member states

1986 The Single European Act (SEA) is signed by Foreign Ministers to come into effect the following year

1987 Turkey applies for EC membership

1989 German monetary union; start of collapse of Communism in Eastern Europe and Austria applies for EC membership

1990 First stage of economic and Monetary Union; Cyprus and Malta apply for EC membership; Re-unification of Germany and former East Germany becomes part of the EU; European year for tourism

1991 Sweden Applies for EC membership; Maastricht European Council agrees the principles of Treaty on European Union (TEU); Yugoslavia begins to break apart

1992 Maastricht Treaty on European Union signed; Finland, Switzerland and Norway apply for membership; Swiss withdrawal of application; European Olympic Year proposal

1993 Treaty on European Union comes into effect, the Single Market is completed with the «four freedoms» of movement of goods, services, people and money; European Year of Older People and Solidarity between Generations

1994 Stage Two of Economic and Monetary Union begins; Hungary and Poland apply for EU membership; Norway referendum rejects EU membership; European Nutrition Year

1995 Austria, Finland and Sweden join the EU, increasing the membership to fifteen states; Romania, the Slovak Republic, Latvia, Estonia, Lithuania and Bulgaria apply for EU membership; the single currency will be called the Euro (not the Ecu); Bosman ruling. The European Court of Justice decrees that football federation rules restricting the number of foreign players in football teams and those relative to players' transfers are contrary to Community law; European Year of Road Safety and Young Drivers

1996 Czech Republic and Slovenia apply for EU membership; European Year for Lifelong Learning

1997 The Commission presents Agenda 2000 – for a stronger and wider Europe, its opinions on the applications of ten central and eastern European countries; European Year against Racism and Xenophobia

1999 The Euro is officially launched: Austria, Belgium, Finland, France, Germany, Ireland, Italy, Luxembourg, The Netherlands, Portugal and Spain adopt the Euro as their official currency

2001 Greece becomes the twelfth member country to join the Euro zone

2002 Euro coins and notes enter into circulation

2004 The EU experiences its largest enlargement in terms of scope and diversity with ten new countries joining: Cyprus, the Czech Republic, Estonia, Hungary, Latvia, Lithuania, Malta, Poland, the Slovak Republic, and Slovenia together represent more than 100 million citizens; the European Year of Education through Sport, EYES 2004, is launched

2007 The accession of Romania and Bulgaria completes the fifth enlargement of the EU to twenty-seven member states and the population within the union to 492.8 million inhabitants. The EU now has 23 official languages, following the addition of Bulgarian, Romanian and Irish; Slovenia successfully adopts the Euro

2009 Serbia applies for EU membership

Appendix 2: Some Key Dates for European Association Football[4]

1857 Creation of Sheffield FC, and formulation of Sheffield rules

1857 Publication of Tom Brown's Schooldays by Thomas Hughes

1863 Formation of the Football Association (FA) in England and 14 Laws of the Game

1871 Formation of Rugby Football Union marks a split in football codes

1872 First Final of the FA Cup; First home international under Association rules England-Scotland (0-0); Havre Athletic Club established

1881 England-Scotland women's international match and subsequent tour

1883 Blackburn Olympic beat Old Etonians (2-1) in the FA Cup, the first team of northern origin to win

1885 Professionalism accepted by the Football Association

1886 First meeting of the International Football Association Board (IFAB) to set the laws of the game comprised of four British Football Associations

1888 Creation of the Football League; foundation of Celtic Football and Glasgow Athletic clubs

1889 Preston North End become the first team to win the 'double' championship of the Football League and FA Cup in the same year

1892 Genoa Football and Cricket Club formed

---

4   Compiled from Patrick Brennan (2010), Christiane Eisenberg, Pierre Lanfranchi, Tony Mason and Alfred Wahl (2004), Jean Williams (2003, 2007) and Paul Dietschy (2010).

1894 The British Ladies Football Club formed in London and go on to play approximately one hundred games between 1895-7; Mrs Graham's Eleven play an addition twenty, many in Scotland and the north of England

1899 FC Barcelona created

1900 Deutscher Fussball Bund (DFB) created

1902 International match between Vienna and Austria Hungary (5-0); Ibrox stadium disaster in Scotland kills twenty-seven people; English FA bars male teams playing against women's teams

1904 Foundation of the Fédération Internationale de Football Association, FIFA in Paris; France play Brussels (3-3)

1908 FA-controlled Olympic football tournament

1911 Reports of women's football in Russia

1912 Eleven male teams play in the Stockholm Olympic Games football tournament

1914 George V becomes the first English King to attend an FA Cup Final; creation of British football battalions under Kitchener

1916 Confederación Sudamericana de Fútbol (CONMEBOL) inaugurated

1917 Growth of «Munitionettes» football and other women's teams in Britain – up to 150 by 1921; growth of women's football teams in France, often as part of gymnastic clubs

1918 First Final of the Charles Simon/French Cup between l'Olympique de Pantin and FC Lyon (2-1)

1920 Belgium win the Olympic tournament in Antwerp; Jules Rimet attends two women's football matches in Paris; British teams withdraw from FIFA; Dick, Kerr Ladies Football Club play matches against French team Femina in Preston

1921 Election of Jules Rimet as president of FIFA; English FA ban women's teams playing on Football League and Football Association-affiliated grounds (rescinded between 1969-1971); First unofficial «Women's Olympic Games» in Paris includes football, basketball and Hanza (Czech handball) alongside track and field athletics

1923 Wembley stadium inaugurated; French and English women's team play matches in Barcelona; Dick, Kerr's Ladies FC play against male professional teams in the United States

1924 Victory for Uruguay over the Swiss (3-0) in the Paris Olympic football tournament; Professionalism accepted in Austria

1927 First edition of the Mitropa Cup won by Sparta Prague; four British associations leave FIFA over the question of amateurism

1928 Second Uruguay victory in an Olympic tournament (2-1 against Argentina) in front of 90,000 spectators; FIFA decides to hold its own tournament; a professional Spanish league is created; Dynamo Moscow stadium inaugurated

1930 First FIFA World Cup won by Uruguay (2-1 against Argentina) in Montevideo in front of 100,000 spectators; Arsenal's FA Cup victory using manager Herbert Chapman's consciously modern methods; around 80 women players are active in Germany, most famously Lotte Specht

1931 First France versus Germany fixture (1-0) and Raoul Diagne becomes the first black player to play for France

1932 Professionalism accepted in France and Uruguay

1933 Professionalism accepted in Brazil; the DFB exclude Jews and workers' sport movement members

1934 Italy host and win the World Cup, beating Czechoslovakia 2-1 in the Final watched by Benito Mussolini

1938 Italian victory at the World Cup staged in France, winning by 4 goals to 2 in the Final against Hungary; England-Germany game at the Olympic stadium Berlin

1942 Brothers Starostin of Spartak Moscow are exiled to Siberia

1945 Dynamo Moscow tour England; Dick, Kerr and Femina teams continue internationals as «England» versus «France»

1946 German and Japanese national associations excluded from FIFA, the return of the British associations

1947 Entry of the Soviet national association to FIFA

1949 First Latin Cup won by FC Barcelona; Superga air disaster involving the death of eighteen Torino AC players (Il Grande Torino) returning from a match in Lisbon

1951 Women's football matches played as part of the Festival of Britain; Manchester Corinthians take the Festival of Britain Trophy

1953 Defeat of England by Hungary (3-6) at Wembley Stadium

1954 Foundation of UEFA with 30 member associations (Albania; Austria; Belgium; Bulgaria; Czechoslovakia; Denmark; England; Finland; France; FR Germany; German DR; Greece; Hungary; Iceland; Ireland Republic; Italy; Luxembourg; Netherlands; Northern Ireland; Norway; Poland; Portugal; Romania; Scotland; Spain; Sweden; Switzerland; USSR; Wales and Yugoslavia); Asian Football Confederation (AFC) formed; Jules Rimet becomes FIFA President; first TV transmission of a World Cup, when West Germany win over Hungary in Switzerland 3-2 in a tournament that set new records for goal-scoring

1955 Creation of the European Club Champions' Cup instigated by *L'Equipe* journalists Gabriel Hanot and Jacques Ferran; the Inter-Cities Fairs Cup is inaugurated by ten teams from April 1955; Turkey join UEFA; the DFB re-state their ban on women's football

1956 Real Madrid win the inaugural European Club Champions' Cup, beating Stade de Reims 4-3 in the Final, held in Paris; following the Hungarian Revolution, a mass migration of players takes place from the country; an unofficial German women's national team win 2-1 over a team representing the Netherlands in Essen

1957 Confédération Africaine de Football (CAF) was founded; an unofficial women's European competition held in Germany involves teams representing Austria, England, Luxembourg, the Netherlands and West Germany

1958 Munich Air Disaster and the death of 8 Manchester United players

1960 Creation of the UEFA European Nations Cup/ Henri-Delauny Cup, to be held in even years between World Cup competitions; Malta join UEFA

1961 Election of Stanley Rous as head of FIFA; the Confederation of North, Central American and Caribbean Association Football (CONCACAF) was created

1963 Bundesliga inaugurated

1964 Cyprus join UEFA

1966 England win the World Cup 4-2 against Germany at Wembley; the Oceania Football Confederation (OFC) is constituted

1967 Celtic become the first British club to win the European Cup after beating Inter Milan 2-1

1968 Manchester United win the European Cup; the Asian Ladies Football Association host their first unofficial «Women's World Cup» competition

1969 FIFA reconsiders its view of women's football; UEFA follows suit

1971 First re-titled UEFA Cup won by Ajax of Amsterdam; FIFA and UEFA issue surveys to all member national associations about the status of women's football; two Italian women's professional leagues recruit international players

1972 West Germany win the European Championship at their first attempt, defeating the Soviet Union 3–0 in the final

1973 Ajax win European Cup for the third consecutive season; after Feyenoord's victory in 1970, this becomes the fourth year in a row that a Dutch team has won

1974 Election of João Havelange to FIFA Presidency; West Germany beat Netherlands 2–1 in the World Cup final at the Olympiastadion in Munich; Liechtenstein join UEFA

1975 Leeds United supporters riot at the final of the European Cup at the Parc des Princes

1976 Bayern Munich win European Cup for third consecutive season

1978 European-wide campaign to boycott the World Cup in Argentina

1979 PR China re-join FIFA

1982 Italy win their third World Cup beating West Germany 3–1 in Spain, Poland are third and France fourth; 340 people die at the Lenin stadium at a match between Spartak Moscow and Dutch club Haarlam; UEFA begin a competition for women's national teams

1984 France win the seventh UEFA European Football Championship held in France, their first major title and Spain are runners up

1985 Thirty-nine Juventus FC fans die at a match between their team and Liverpool FC at Heysel stadium Brussels

1986 The Maradona «Hand of God» incident at Argentina's 2-1 victory over England in the World Cup quarter finals at the Estadio Azteca in Mexico City. Maradona's second goal was later voted Goal of the Century by FIFA.com; Argentina went on to beat West Germany by three goals to two in the Final

1988 San Marino join UEFA

1989 Ninety-six spectators die at the Hillsborough stadium disaster in Sheffield

1990 The Faroe Islands join UEFA

1991 The first Women's World Champsionship in PR China is contested by twelve national associations and won by the United States who beat Norway by two goals to one in the Final; Sweden beat Germany by four goals to nil to take third place

1992 Satellite company BSkyB sign a £300 million contract to televise the newly-formed Premier League; Estonia, Latvia and Lithuania join UEFA

1993 Armenia, Belarus, Croatia, Georgia, Slovenia and Ukraine join UEFA; creation of the men's professional «J» League in Japan

1994 Brazil win the World Cup USA '94 in the United States to take the title for the fourth time; Italy are second, Sweden third and Bulgaria fourth; Azerbaijan, Israel, Macedonia, Moldova and Slovakia join UEFA

1995 Second Women's World Cup is held in Sweden in conjunction with an athletics meeting, Norway defeat Germany by two goals to one in the Final; the Bosman case challenges «quota systems» for the transfer of foreign players

1996 The first Olympic competition for women's football is held in Atlanta, breaking new record for spectator attendance with over 70,000 fans watching the United States beat PR China by two goals to one in the Final; Andorra joins UEFA

1997 First UEFA U18 Women's tournament

1998 Bosnia and Herzegovina join UEFA

1999 The third Women's World Cup in United States of America is extended to sixteen national associations, breaking new records for live spectator attendance and media coverage; 93,000 supporters attend the Final

2000 Sydney hosts the second Olympic women's football tournament where Norway beat the United States in the Final by three goals to two, becoming the only European team to hold an Olympic Gold; Women's United Soccer Association (WUSA) professional league is launched in the United States

2002 Kazakhstan joins UEFA; First FIFA Women's U19 tournament

2003 The fourth Women's World Cup is relocated to the United States due to an outbreak of SARS virus in the PR China, Germany beat Sweden by two goals to one in the Final; WUSA suspends operations

2004 Athens hosts the third Olympic women's football tournament, the United States beat Brazil by two goals to one in the Final; Germany and Sweden finish third and fourth

2007 Montenegro joins UEFA; PR China host the fifth Women's World Cup, Germany win the title for a second time by beating Brazil by two goals to nil in the Final; First UEFA U17 Women's tournament

2008 Beijing hosts the fourth Olympic women's football tournament, the United States beat Brazil by one goal to nil in the Final; Germany win their third successive bronze medal by defeating Japan 2-0 in the third place playoffs; a Women's Professional Soccer league relaunch begins (WPS); First FIFA Women's U17 tournament

2010 World Cup in South Africa; U20 Women's World Cup Germany; U17 Women's World Cup Trinidad and Tobago

2011 Launch of Women's Super League; the sixth FIFA Women's World Cup Germany is won by Japan after they beat the United States in a penalty shoot out; Sweden and France take third and fourth place; WPS suspends operations

2012 London hosts the fifth Olympic women's football tournament in which the United States take the gold medal for the fourth time, defeating the World Cup holders, Japan in the Final by two goals to one. Allocation for each continent is set at: Europe 3 (including hosts Great Britain); Africa 2; Asia 2; South America 2; North America 2 and Oceania 1

2015 The schedule for the seventh Women's World Cup in Canada is extended to twenty-four national associations

2015 The sixth Olympic Women's football tournament will be hosted in Rio de Janeiro, Brazil

Appendix 3: Summary of the European-wide growth in women's football 1996-2003, by national association

This summary used the available surveys into the status of women's football in European national associations to provide a comparative review. These range between the *1974 UEFA questionnaire* (the earliest available) and the *2003 FIFA survey* (the latest) to begin to map out European-wide developments. The sources comprise: *UEFA Survey on women's football in 1974* (correspondence, agendas, personal notes, newspaper articles, questionnaires); UEFA Survey on women's football in 1985 (mainly comprised of questions on player numbers); *UEFA Questionnaire on women's football in 1996* (player numbers; league structures; national association control; administration arrangements and areas of women's football development); *FIFA Survey Circular 609 on status of women's football in 1997* (player numbers; league structures; national teams at each level; women's refereeing/coaches); *FIFA Women's Football Research in 2003* (player numbers; league structures; national association administration, women's football development) and the *UEFA Questionnaire on Domestic Women's Leagues in 2003* (player numbers; league structures; national association control; administration arrangements; areas of women's football development and suggestions for how UEFA could help). The information from 1974 and 1985 has largely been incorporated into the main body of the report and so is not expressly summarised here. I have used it mainly to indicate where a national association was part of the nascent women's football community before FIFA and UEFA recognition. Future researchers will also be able to use the *UEFA Club Licensing Survey* conducted in 2008. This concerned proposals for a Club Licensing System for top division women's leagues and was sent to the forty-four associations with clubs participating in the 2007/8 UEFA Women's Cup. Twenty-six replies were received but the information was embargoed at the time of my visit in 2011.

Questionnaires are only as good as their design, communication and completion. Sometimes, depending on time, circumstance and personnel, the information for a given national association contradicted previous surveys or contrasted with other information in the public domain. Some evidence continuity of personnel and others show different voices in the completed questionnaires. Where this is the case, and when possible, I have presented who completed the information and at what date. For some examples the questionnaires were completed annonymously, so only the date is given. Some are also undated. Where a national association was surveyed according to the records but did not return the questionnaire a nil-return (N/R) is registered. Any interpretation in this summary belongs to the person who completed the questionnaire. The data is not neatly comparative and I chose to reflect the problemmatic nature of the source material rather than to sanitise it by drawing up tables in order to regularise the information. It contains multiple and overlapping perspectives therefore which, in a project of this scale, I thought it important to reflect. The questions asked by the governing bodies reflected their priorities; the respondees do not necessarily share those same views. Consequently, this is a somewhat «official» view of women's football and if the grassroots supporter who facilitates play week-in, week-out had been surveyed, the results would no doubt have been different. Nevertheless, some of those individuals are also represented here.

There are two important caveats to this provisional material, which is intended to supplement the main body of the report, rather than reflect a definitive snapshot of the women's game in its entirety. Firstly, some countries, particularly Germany, England, France, the Netherlands and some Scandiavian examples are treated more briefly than might be expected. They have been more widely discussed in the main body of the argument. In addition, their histories have already been extensively developed in discrete academic works, and if incorporated here would have run to many pages and therefore distort the attempt at an overview. Secondly, there were many other surveys, so this country-by-country analysis is indicative of how the work might be further developed. It is an attempt at an inclusive map of European women's soccer but the gaps will be all too apparent. It can do no more than begin to summarise European-wide developments from previously uncollated documentation. Taken as a whole, this material supports the thesis made in the body of the project. The widely amateur nature of European women's football in the late twentieth century is indicated by player status, by administrative voluntarism, by an under-developed infrastructure and by limited financial support plus attendant under-exposed commercialisation of the women's game.

Albania   *joined UEFA 1954*

(N/R) to surveys 1974; 1996; 1997; FIFA 2003; UEFA 2003 and no attendance at UEFA conference for women's football held in London, England 27-30 October 1998.

Andorra   *joined UEFA 1996*

(N/R) 1996; no attendance at UEFA conference for women's football held in London, England 27-30 October 1998.

1997 FIFA Survey Circular 609 completed by Christian D'Argueyrolles 17 May 1997. «Women's Football has existed since 1997 in Andorra with no previous evidence of interest in women's sport, though 3 women work in the national association. There are a total of 37 registered players, 100% of which were beginners/amateurs. Andorra would like national and international competitions to stimulate growth».

2003 FIFA survey Circular 871-no name and undated. «Women's football has existed since 1997, mainly amongst amateur girls with 43 players».

2003 UEFA Questionnaire on Domestic Women's Leagues-no name and undated. Fifty six registered women players took part in in four teams; the playing season ran between October to May plus there were an unspecified number of under 14 and under 17 participants, all amateur.

Armenia   *joined UEFA 1993*

1996 UEFA Questionnaire response by S. Navasardian, Youth Football Department, was a letter dated 14 May 1996. The letter reported no national championship in Yerevan but some participation by three groups of girls aged twelve and thirteen years old. The Armenian national association hoped to have women's football in the future.

1997 FIFA Survey Circular 609 covering letter from Pavel Khacha-
tryan, General Secretary of the Football Federation of Armenia 21 May
1997. «There is no women's football at any level and this information
is final».

No attendance at UEFA conference for women's football held in England 27-30 October 1998.

(N/R) FIFA 2003 Circular 871.

2003 UEFA Questionnaire on Domestic Women's Leagues-no name no
date. The League operates between 25 April to 31 October each year
and there was one division comprised of four clubs who played 12
matches, mostly on Sundays. There was also a Championship for local
colleges.

Austria   *joined UEFA 1954*

1996 UEFA Questionnaire response by Alfred Ludwig GS of Österrei-
chischer Fussball-Bund 5 March 1996. Seventy-one official women's
and girls' teams were reported. The overall number of participants by
age-groups were: Under 12, 998; 12-16, 1000; 16-20, 980; over 20,
2,540. Women's and girls' football was integrated into the national association and overseen by Sepp Pösinger, with the season lasting September to June. There were eight regional leagues, the largest four of
which were: Steiermark (14 teams); Salzburg (7), Vorarlberg (12) Bur-
genland (12). The First Division was won in 1994/5 season by USC
Landhaus, Wien (Vienna) and the Cup by Union Kleinmünchen. All
the players were amateur and the First Division clubs were: Union
Kleinmünchen; USC Landhaus; DFC Heindenreichstein; ASV Vösen-
dorf; ESV Südost; 1 DFC Leoben; SC Neunkirchen and FC Vienna.
Second Division clubs were: DFC Obersdorf; SV Altlengbach; ATSV
Deutsch-Wagram; SC Brunn; SV Horn; SV Donau; DFV Juwelen Ja-
necka and DFC Pellendorf.

1997 FIFA Survey Circular 609 (no covering letter) «Austria has had
women's football since 1968 and it has been recognised by the national
association since 1971. Two women administrators were reported and

there was a Bundesliga with 6 teams, and a second division with 10 clubs». In addition there were regional and junior leagues, all reported as 100% amateur, with junior participation from 10-13 and 10-14. There were two women A licence coaches; three with mid-range and five with lower qualifications. The Austrian national association asked for more help in attracting sponsorship, more media coverage and an increased number of competitions.

2003 FIFA survey Circular 871 letter-headed Umfrage Frauenfussball Fragenbogen für Nationalverbände Austria, response 23 September 2003. «Women's football has been organised within the national association since 1982. It has been known in Austria since 1935 but the Austrian FA intervened in 1973 because of the interest of profit-seeking groups and individuals. In 1973 approximately 18 teams played in organised competitions, hence the need for supra-regional competitions where 400 to 500 players participated and some international awareness developed. There were no national teams in 1973 as there were only 18 teams. There were no professional and no semi-professional players in 2003».

«Ten amateur teams have competed in the Bundesliga since 1982 with a further 34 playing in a second division from 1999 onwards. Junior (under 15s) teams have been developed from 1999 onwards with some mixed football». A national team has existed since 1990 and the best clubs were USC Landhaus; Union Kleinmünden and Lechen, SV Neulengbach. Key personnel were: Ernst Weber, Team Chief; Tito Spindler, Team Manager A and U19 squads and Renado Gligorosla. The committee for women's football oversaw the development of national and international teams. Development priorities for 2003 included schools football for boys and girls.

2003 UEFA Questionnaire on Domestic Women's Leagues-no name undated. In Austria, the season was played from the end of August until the end of June. There were three divisions and ten teams in the top flight, competing in about 25 matches annually, with most games played on Saturdays and Sundays. Although there were national and cup matches, 100% of the players were amateur. The minimum age for youth olayers range from 4 years old to 15.

Azerbaijan   *joined UEFA 1994*

(N/R) 1996.

1997 FIFA Survey Circular 609 completed by Fuad Musayev, President of Association of Football Federations of Azerbaijan, (AFFA) 42 Hussi Hajievstr, 370009 Baku, Azerbaijan on 13 May 1997. «Women's Football in our country has developed from 1986. Three women's football teams were organised and they successfully played at the championship of the USSR until 1990. After the Soviet Union was disintegrated, Women's Football in the Republic stopped its cultivation (sic). The reason was the departure of the Russian-speaking population to the other republics, which had previously provided the main staff of the team. The majority of leading players started their activity in the best women's teams of Turkey and Russia, under the supervision of AFFA. At the current time, AFFA undertakes the necessary measures of cultivation for women's football in the Republic. That is why the Federation of Women's Football was created, and now it makes efforts to create new women's teams, the hosting of our country's championship and the functions of a women's national team in the Republic».

No attendance from at UEFA conference for women's football held in London, England 27-30 October 1998.

2003 FIFA survey Cricular 871-no name and undated. Some of the five teams and 50 adult players appear to have participated in the USSR championship between 1980 and 1990, the Azerbaijan federation has taken control of women's football since 1997. Five women worked on committees; there was no national league; no top players; no internationals; no referees; no tv coverage and elementary participation otherwise. The prospects for women's football, though, were assessed as positive.

2003 UEFA Questionnaire on Domestic Women's Leagues Azerbaijan May-July 1 division 5/6 clubs who play 20/5 games mostly on Saturdays and Sundays plus international women's day cup competition 50:50 semi pro amateur. Min age 15.

Belarus   *joined UEFA 1993*

1996 UEFA Questionnaire response by Alexander Gursky President The Football Federation of the Republic of Belarus 29 Febraury 1996. Gursky reported that, even with economic difficulties, interest among women and girls was growing. There were twenty-four registered teams catering for 450-500 players. Total participation rates by age group were: Under 12, 70; 12-16, 140; 16-20, 140 and over 20, 100 players. A separate Belarus Association of Women's Football was responsible for development and one woman, Belkevich Yelens, was on the Executive Committee. The season was played May to the end of September. There was no regular championship. There were ten teams in the first division and fourteen in the second. The 1994/5 season League Champions were FC Victorian-86, Brest and the Cup winners were Belcar Bobruisk. For the 1995/6 season, the highest division included: FC Victorian-86, Brest; Nadezhda-Spartak, Mogilev; Electronika-Elinta, Minsk; Universitie Vitebsk; Slavianka Bobruisk; Yunost Mogilev; Nika Brest; Gloria Kobrin and Titan Grodno. Semiprofessionals comprised 40% and amateurs 60% of the total number of female players. League entry fees were $200 and a minimum age of 15 for senior competitions. School football was arranged at city level in the Republic and at city district level in Minsk,Mogilev, Bobruisk and Brest. The European Championship was important to attract more girls, as were friendly-internationals, most recently with Poland, Germany and France.

2003 UEFA Questionnaire on Domestic Women's Leagues completed by Valery Yakunin, Head of Women's Football Department, Belarus FootballFederation 8/2 Kirov Street Minsk 220030, 24 September 2003. Womens football in Belarus had expanded steadily. There were 80 registered players in 1990; 140 in 1995; 210 in 2000; 270 in 2003. The playing season was April to October. There have been league matches since 1992 and a Belarus Championship since 1995. There had been eight semi professional clubs active since 1992. The most well known teams are Bobruichanka; Nadezhda and Vitebsk. The national team aspired to play in Euro competitions as an important means of raising their international profile.

2003 FIFA survey Circular 871 response by Valrey Ykunin, Head of Women's Football Department, 8/2/ Kirov Street Minsk 220030, 31 October 2003. Women's football was organised by the BFF since 1992: women have their own football association and players can get a licence at age 16. In 1990 the BFF licensed 80 players; in 1995, 140 players; in 2000, 210 players and in 2003, 270 players. The unlicensed estimates were, in 1990, 40; in 1995, 70; in 2000, 110 and in 2003, 120 plus players. At under 16 level there were 150 particpants. The season runs from April to October with eight semi-professional clubs in theleague of the Belarus Championship. There have been no mixed football since 1992. There have been youth competitions for seven teams, each at 15-16 and 14-15 age-levels since 1995. There has been a Belarus Open and U19 competition since 1995. There are a national and under 19 national team. Euro 2007 qualification was important for the national squad.

The most successful teams were Bobruichanka, Nadezhda, Vitebsk and in 2003 Bobruichanka were champions. Spectators for national games have ranged between 500 in the year 2000 and 2,000 in 2003 with an average of 1500; league games attracted crowds of 500-1000 supporters with an average of 750 per game. Some games were transmitted on national TV channels and local stations. The press covered national team matches often and sponsorship, in the form of financial support and equipment, was provided by Belinvestbank, Elitasport. Developments were supported by the State budget and the women's FA. Development priorities were girls' football lessons in schools with an expected spend of US $70-100,000 per year. The federation had fifty-two staff of whom 37 are employed and 15 were volunteers. There was one employee for women's football and four volunteers: Sergei Safarian Vice (President); Valery Yakunin (chairman of women's committee); Mikhail Andruzheichik; Gennaoly Pashevich and Irina Bulygina (all memebers of the women's committee). They had responsibility for all women's football matters, except refereeing. There were no plans to involve more women in the association but there were plans to develop female coaching. The respondee thought that FIFA was doing well in regular tournaments and awareness-raising days.

Belgium   *joined UEFA 1954*

1996 UEFA Questionnaire response Alain Courtois, Secretary General of the Belgian national association, 5 May 1996. Belgium had increased women's and girls' participation in that last five years to the grand total of total 11,066, which was broken down by the following age groups: Under 12, 2,113 players; 12-16, 1,637; 16-20, 1,637 and above 20 years of age, 5,679. Madame B. Vandelannoote was President of commission for women's football: all five people on the commission were women. The season ran from September to June. The current League Champions were Anderlecht, and the Cup winners that year Standard Fémina de Liège. All players were amateurs. There were four national teams at the following age-bands: Adult, U21, U16 and U14. There were no special coaching courses for women and around 80 female referees.

1997 FIFA Survey Circular 609 completed by J Peeters, Secretary General of the Belgian national association, 5 June 1997. «Belgium has had women's football since 1971 when it was first recognised and since then it has been administered by the national association». There were five female representatives on a women's commission of six individuals. There was one national league with two divisions and seven provincial leagues. Players were 100% amateur. The Under 21 and Under 16 teams played, on average, three national team matches per season.

2003 FIFA survey Circular 871 response by Jean-Paul Hoben, Secretary General Union Royale Belge des Sociétés de Football Association, Av. Houba De Strooper 145, 1020 Bruxelles, 18 November 2003. Women's football had been organised under the national association since 1971 and a girl could obtain a licence at 5 years old. By 1973 there were 100 teams and 2,000 women playing in a first division (of the 14 best teams) and a second-level competition (of nine provinces) for a regional championship. In 1990 there were around 8,000 licensees; in 1995, 10,620; in 2000, 15,486 and in 2003, 20,014 and an additional 7,507 at under 16 level. The number of unlicensed players was not known. A separate appendix showed 57 autonomous clubs in 1988 and 48 in 2003 with female sections of male clubs since 1995 starting at 100 and totalling in 156 by 2003. The playing season ran from mid August to the end of May each year.

2003 UEFA Questionnaire on Domestic Women's Leagues There had been no professional or semi-professional female players since 1971 and the Coupe de Belgique, run since 1976, was intended for amateurs. There had been mixed football for juniors up to 14 since 1997. A senior and junior league and national team had been organised since 1979. The best teams were KSC Eendracht Aalst; Rapide Wezemall and RSC Anderlecht. In 2003 the champions were SK Lebke Aalst. The current national teams were at senior, U19 and U17 levels. There was little coverage on television and in the press, though Nike sometimes sponsored equipment. The key objectives for development included talent identification and a diploma for coaches and trainers. The national association expected to spend 110,600 Euros in the 2002/3 season. Of the 150 people employed by the association (plus 100 volunteers), 2 employees and 20 volunteers ran women's football. Nathalie Bosmans was the secretary of the commission for women's football. The women's committee was responsible for the development of the league. Other initiatives, like the national team, belong to the technical committee, the central refereeing committee, the medical committee and the school committee. There was no discrete provision for female administrators. Other priority developments included regional structures. The respondee asked for help in communication between FIFA and UEFA, and saw Belgium in the first phase of development.

Bosnia-Herzegovina   joined UEFA in 1998

1997 FIFA Survey Circular 609 completed by Mr Miso Bogdan, President of the Commission for Women's Football, 12 May 1997. Bosnia and Herzegovina has had football for past twenty years and women have been part of the association since 1994. Until 1992 female players and teams participated in the highest leagues in Yugoslavia. Slow development was reported because of the war and working conditions. The football federation of Bosnia and Herzegovina established a commission for women's football in 1994. A national league with 6 teams was reported, with the players 100% amateur. There was one national team, but there had been no regular play against other national teams. For 30% of women's teams there was a woman coach and a further two female teachers were qualified as coaches. While private companies were said to sponsor women's teams, no names or examples were given.

2003 FIFA survey Circular 871 anonymous, undated. Women's football has been played since 1968 and was integrated in 1996 within the FFBH i.e. organised within the national association. Players could get a licence at age 15 and the total in 2003 was 27 players. The season ran from May to June and eight amateur clubs compete with players aged 15-35. There was no mixed soccer.

2003 UEFA Questionnaire on Domestic Women's Leagues anonymous, undated. A national league with eight teams was reported, with the players 100% amateur. There was one national team, but there had been no regular play against other national teams. There was a woman coach and a further two female teachers were qualified as coaches. Private companies were said to sponsor women's teams but no names were given.

Bulgaria   *joined UEFA in 1954*

1996 UEFA Questionnaire response by Bontcho Todorov Secretary International BFU Karnigradska 19 1000 Sofia, 28 Feb 1996. Five teams catered for approximately 280 players: of this total, by age group, the numbers were broken down as Under 12, 90; 12-16, 60; 16-20, 65 and over 20, 65. A women's football committee oversaw developments and there was a female administrator. Fewer than ten per cent of players were professional, the rest amateur.

1997 FIFA Survey Circular 609 and *2003 FIFA survey Circular 871* both anonymous, undated. Women's football was integrated into the national association in 1996. There were 200 players under sixteen years of age and 300 registered adult participants. There was an amateur national league of five teams: FC «Grand Hotel Varna»; Locomotiv Stara Zagora; CSKA; NSA and Septemvri.

2003 UEFA Questionnaire on Domestic Women's Leagues anonymous, undated. There was a commision of women's football and one woman administrator worked at the national association. Eight per cent of female players were professional and the rest were amateurs. School football only existed in Varna. FC «Grand Hotel Varna» had organised an international tournament since 1996 and there was one female

international-standard referee. Emil Atanassov was the Women's national team head coach and Latchezar Dimitrov Vice President of the
women's commission.

Croatia   *joined UEFA in 1993*

1996 UEFA Questionnaire completed by Josip Cop GS CFF Zagreb 6
March 1996. There were five clubs with a total of 150 registered players. Broken down by age group they were as follows: between the ages
of 16-20, there were 60 participants and over 20 years of age, there
were 90 players. The main contact for the women's football committee
was Mrs Ivancica Sudac-Junaci, who also acted as the international
secretary. There was one woman on the Executive Committee. The
women's football season began in September and and finished in May
each year. The five main clubs for 1995/6 season were: ZNK Elektro
Osijek from Osijeck; ZNK Maksimir-Trgometal, Zagreb; ZNK Loto,
Zagreb; ZNK Susedgread, Zagreb and ZNK Viktorija Slavoknski Brod
with ZNK Elektro Osijek winning both the national league and the cup.
All players were amateur. There were no junior and only friendly international matches, but UEFA competitions were thought to be important
networking opportunities.

1997 FIFA Survey Circular 609 (no covering letter). Croatia has had
women's football since 1937 and the committee for women's football
had been part of the federation since 1972 but economic and conflict
difficulties had made continuity difficult. Two of the five members of
the women's committee were female. There was a Croation championship for women's teams and a cup competition for five clubs. All
women players were amateur and totalled approximately 175 registered participants. The national team competed for Euro championship
qualifiers. No further details were provided on coaches and referees.
Some sponsors were reported as private firms. New circumstances of
peace and improved economic conditions were encouraging for the
growth of the women's game.

2003 FIFA questionnaire Circular 871 and *2003 UEFA Questionnaire
on Domestic Women's Leagues* both anonymous, undated. There was
a national championship for ten women's teams and a cup competition

for all clubs. All players were amateur and totalled approximately 250 registered participants. The main aim of the national association was the development of youth leagues and a five year development plan for women's football. No further details were provided on domestic coaches and refereees. Damir Ruhek was the women's national team and U19 squad head coach; Alan Balen was a Women's League Committee member.

Cyprus   *joined UEFA in 1964*

1996 UEFA Questionnaire letter response from Andreas Stylianou, Manager of the Cyprus Football Association Nicosia, 7 February 1996. The national association did not organise women's football.

1997 FIFA Survey Circular 609 letter Andreas Stylinaou, CFA manager Stasinos Street Engorni 2404 Nicosia PO Box 5071, 2 June 1997. The letter reported no women's football and no association/ commission.

2003 FIFA questionnaire Circular 871 and *2003 UEFA Questionnaire on Domestic Women's Leagues* both anonymous, undated. There were now 100 registered women players, all amateurs. Chrysostomos Ikovou had become the women's national team head coach and Tassos Katsikides the Chair of the women's Football Committee. There were plans to host an invitational tournament to stimulate interest in women's football.

Czechoslovakia/Czech Rep.   *joined UEFA in 1954*

1996 UEFA Questionnaire completed by Petr Fousek, International Secretary Football Association of Czech Republic, 19 May 1996. Prof Dr V. Minarovjech had represented Czechoslovakia at UEFA/ FIFA conferences on women's football from 1980. A «restrained optimism» was reported with 59 clubs catering for the following numbers of players: 12-16, 438; 16-20, 759 and over 20, 1,643. All were amateurs. Otto Beichel was Chairman of the Committee for Women's Football and Sarka Novotna was Committee Secretary. The season ran from September to the end of April each year. There was a national division of 12 clubs and a second division of 9-10 teams. League champions were Sparta Praha, there was no national cup competition. There was a senior national team only and one female referee, Mrs Damkova.

1997 FIFA questionnaire Circular 609 completed by Dr Zdenek Sivek Director Diskarska 100 169 00 Praha. Women's football had been recognised since the 1960s and female players had been affiliated to national association since 1985. The committee Chaired was Mr Beichel. There were two women of the eight member committee (all were voluntary workers, not employees). There was a national first division with 12 teams and two second divisions with 8 teams in each. One of these was based in Bohemia and one in Moravia; both the winners from Bohemia and from Moravia get promoted to the first division. There were also indoor junior leagues. There were fewer than 1,700 registered female players in total and all were amateur. There had been one club international player and about 10% of women's teams had female coaches. 2 referees. «Czech society realises that the promotion of women's sports, particularly football is the cheapest prevention against some of the ills of our time (poor health, drugs) and also a pre requisite for the best sports development in general (mother and child, raised in the sport-orientated environment). Traits like ability to co operate with other people, straightforwardness and so on are usually important in sport-orientated families. From a health point of view, generally sport contributes to the development of women's health and consequently of their offspring, which forms a potential pool of quality sportsmen and women. The equation minimal financing=maximal effect sums up the opinion of relevant sporting bodies. It means that the costs of women's football are minimal and the result is the influx of a new generation of sportswomen [sic]».

2003 FIFA questionnaire Circular 871 and *2003 UEFA Questionnaire on Domestic Women's Leagues* both anonymous. «Women's football started in the sixties without the involvement of the official football bodies and was not regulated in any way. Girls just pulled on the jerseys and went to play. Only after long years, when women's football was taken under the protective wings of the football association were concepts like lifestyle, nutrition or hygiene developed. Girls just took the ball and went to play». There was a national first division, regional leagues and plans for more junior football. Some players played in Slovakian teams with about 200 registered overall. Jan Vejmelka chaired the Women's Football Committee and Dusan Zovinec was women's national team head coach.

Denmark *joined UEFA in 1954*

1996 UEFA Questionnaire completed by Jorgen Hermansen, Secretary of the Dansk Boldspil-Union Brondby, 4 March 1996. Approximately 40,000 female players were registered as active in 2,300 teams, with just over half, almost 25,000, aged between 12 and 16 years of age. Denmrk first had female football in 1964 when it was run by women until the Danish FA took over in 1972. The Danish FA was responsible for development and employed three women. The season ran from the end of March to the end of October each year. for clubs. There was no female school-age football in Denmark. The playing pyramid comprised an elite division, two national first divisions, with 8 teams in each, and other regional leagues. There were 60 female referees active, of whom 9 officiated in the Elite division.

1997 FIFA Survey Circular 609 response by Jorgen Hermansen, General Secretary of the Dansk Boldspil-Union Brondby, 12 May 1997. Denmark has had women's football from 1950 and it has been recognised by the national association since 1972. There was a women's committee of which three members were female and one woman was on the Executive Committee. There was a national female league with eight teams and a second division, then regional leagues with 12 teams, plus 6 local union competitions. The national association organised youth team competitions and the national team took part in the Algarve Cup and Nordic Cup competition. Two women were qualified as top category coaches; there were 60 female referees and 75% of female matches were refereed by women. Sponsorship was provided by insurance company TOPDANMARK.

2003 FIFA questionnaire Circular 871 and *2003 UEFA Questionnaire on Domestic Women's Leagues* (no covering letters). C Nielsen; E Christensen and E Hyldstrup had been part of UEFA's committee to discuss women's football since 1980, when Denmark already had

26,000 female players. Fortuna Hjorring were the current holders of the league, cup and indoor championship titles. Other elite teams were Hjortshoj-Ega; Rodovre; Vejle Boldlub; Odense Boldklub; Brondby IF; Kolding Boldklub and AC Ballerup. All female players were registered as amateurs but about 15 played in other European countries for clubs. About the same number of overseas women played in the elite of Danish clubs. There was now female school-age football in Denmark and youth teams were being developed. The national association had, for many years, organised the Algarve Cup in Portugal, together with Sweden, Norway, Portugal, in which eight nations take part. In addition, the Nordic Cup was also organised between Finland, Norway, Sweden and Denmark. Peter Bonde was the women's national team head coach and Gitte Therkelsen Women's Under 17 and under 19 national team administrator.

England   *joined UEFA in 1954*

1996 UEFA Questionnaire completed by Helen Jevons, Women's Football Co-ordinator, 27 February 1996. The early 1990s saw unprecedented growth growth from 263 teams and about 4,000 participants in 1989 to 500 for 1994/5 with 8,000 registered players. The women's football committee was established in 1993 which employed three regional directors [North, Midlands and South], in addition to a secretary for the Women's Premier League. There was one female on the FA council. The season ran from Sept to April each year. The Premier League winners were Arsenal and other clubs in the elite division were Croydon, Doncaster Belles, Everton, Ilkeston Town Rangers, Liverpool FC, Millwall Lionesses, Villa Aztecs, Wembley and Wolverhampton Wanderers. Arsenal won the Women's FA Cup that year and Wimbledon the League Cup. All female players were amateurs.

1997 FIFA Survey Circular 609 response by Helen Jevons, Women's Football Co-ordinator, 31 March 1997. Women's football in England went back to 1900. Growth from 263 teams in 1989 to 500 for 1994/5 with 8,000 registered players. The FA took over from WFA in 1993. There were three female development staff and a women's co-ordinator. Two female coaches had obtained the Level 4, A License, certificate. The FA planned to host a conference on women's football in 1998.

2003 FIFA questionnaire Circular 871 and *2003 UEFA Questionnaire on Domestic Women's Leagues* Hope Powell had been the women's national team head coach since 1998; Kelly Simmons was Head of Football Development and Susan Hough was an FA Council member. Due to the development of five year plans for women's football, a business case could be made for drawing down funds from a wider range of sources. By 2003 a total of £11.5 million had been spent on women's football, plus a further £60 million into grassroots football generally, especially at youth level. This had mainly come from the FA; Premier League and government funding leveraged through health, crime, drugs, education, community cohesion and social deprivation. There was a coach mentoring scheme. Seven million women were interested in football; almost 150,000 women and girls played football at least once in the last 12 months. From research, 61% of the public were aware of Women's Premier League and 46% had watched women's football on TV. The UEFA 2005 competition would become the first major event in England.

Estonia   *joined UEFA in 1992*

1996 UEFA Questionnaire; 2003 FIFA questionnaire Circular 871 and *2003 UEFA Questionnaire on Domestic Women's Leagues* completed by Mark Tarmak, Estonian Football Association Vice President and General Secretary, undated. The first championship for women had been held in 1994 and since then there had been growing interest. From 1996 to 2003 seven female teams with about 220 players had grown to ten female teams with almost 300 players. No adult women were involved. At the youth level 75 players were under 12; 112 participants were in the 12-16 age group and 33 registrations were in the 16-20 category. The season ran from the end of July to mid-October and mid-April to the end of June with a winter break. There were low numbers of school-age football for both boys and girls but this was an area of priority. The female national team played in Nordic tournaments. There was one woman coach, Lea Ilves, from Tulevik Vilandi. The best teams were Central Pärnu; JK Tulevik Viljandi; Chikens Nõmme and SK Arsenal Lasnamäe. The highest scorers were Aire Lepik the Tulevik number 12 (also player of the year 1994 and 1995); Kaire Kaljurand, the Arsenal number 6; Kristlin Põbb, the Central number

4 and Marje Rannu also a player for Tulevik. By 2003, Jüri Saar was women's national team head coach and Ülli Jurkatamm the head of the competition department.

Faroe Islands   *joined UEFA 1990*

1996 UEFA Questionnaire; *2003 FIFA questionnaire Circular 871* and *2003 UEFA Questionnaire on Domestic Women's Leagues* completed by Isak Mikladal, General Secretary The Faroe Islands' FA Tórshavn, undated. Women's football started in 1985 with 45 teams. It grew to 108 sides in 1990 and 104 in 1992, with a subsequent decrease to 88 teams in 1995. The breakdown of female participants by age groups was: 546 players in 39 Under 12 teams; 480 participants in 32 teams aged between 12-17 and 334 members in 14 teams over 17 years of age. In 1996 there was no separate committee or association and no women on the Executive Committee. However, by 2003 there were promising developments in the country at youth level especially. The season ran from March to September each year. There was a national first division of eight teams from which one was relegated to the second division annually. Generally the second division had between 6 and eight teams each year, plus further regional leagues. At the 14-17 age band 12 teams were divided into two groups and at the 12-14 age band, more than 20 teams were divided into north, east, mid, west and south groupings, all of which played on artificial grass. The domestic champions in 1996 were Havnar Bóltfelag HB of Tórshavn and second division leaders were Leirvikar Itrottarfelag LIF of Leirvik. In the 14-17 age group, Tofta Itrottarfelag of Toftir were winners. Euro competitions were the first internationals of their kind in the country but there many friendly matches against Iceland, Scotland and Westfalia of Germany. In 2003 Alvur Hansen was the women's national team head coach and Karl Videeldt was a board member.

Finland   *joined UEFA in 1954*

1996 UEFA Questionnaire completed by Pertti Alaja Football Association of Finalnd General Secretary 27 February 1996; *1997 FIFA Survey Circular 609* anonymous response; *2003 FIFA questionnaire Circular*

871 and *2003 UEFA Questionnaire on Domestic Women's Leagues* (no covering letters). Women's football had been played in Finland since 1971 and it was recognised by and integrated into the national association's activities from 1972 onwards. There had been good growth from 3,000 female players in 1980, to around 8,000 players in 1994 and 10,000 in 1996. There were 327 teams catering for up to 4,952 female players in the 12-16 age category; 3,382 participants aged between 16 and 20 years of age and 699 adults. Ms Outi Saarinen was the international secretary but there were no other women administrators. The season started in April and ran til the end of October each year. There were ten clubs in the national first division; twenty in the second division and third divisions with 6-8 groups of 10 teams in each. The Finnish Champions for 1995 were Helsingen Jalkapalloklubi (HJK) and the Cup winners were FC Kontu who were also the indoor champions. The top clubs were HJK, FC Kontu, PU-62, MPS, PuiU, Ives, Pyrkivä, FC United, TiPS and SeMi. All female players were amateurs. The national team was sponsored by the Finnish Post Company, who invested 1 million FIM annually in national football teams. In addition, local tournaments had been sponsored by Snickers and Coca-Cola. Helsingin Sanomat, the biggest daily newspaper in Finland, covered some of the international games.

By 2003 there were around 12,000 players and 13 women administrators active across 14 committees. The national first division had 10 teams and a feeder division of 24 teams, split into 2 regional groupings for the north and south. In addition, 30 district-organised teams played in lower divisions. Elite players numbered 206, though all were considered amateur. There were 10-15 overseas players in the national league in Finland, mainly from Norway, USA and England. There was a national team plus youth squads at U21; U19 and U17 level since 1996. Home national games had about 29,000 supporters and league games less. There was one female Pro level coach; one at Advanced level; three in mid level and 80 plus women referees. Michael Käld was the women's national team head coach and Jarmo Matikainen women's under 17 and under 19 national team coach and technical director.

2005 Fifth UEFA Women's Football Conference Oslo Norway 17-19 October 2005 Giorgio Marchetti presented a paper on UEFA's role in developing women's football. At the Women's Euro 2005 competition, hosted in England there had been 117,000 in total stadium attendance. The 29,092 fans at the England v Finland game at the City of Manchester Stadium was a new European record for women's football.

France   *joined UEFA 1954*

1996 UEFA Questionnaire completed by G. Enault, Director General French Football Federation, 23 Feb 1996; *1997 FIFA Survey Circular 609* response by Elisabeth Loisel and Marilou Duringer FFF amateur division undated; *2003 FIFA questionnaire Circular 871* and *2003 UEFA Questionnaire on Domestic Women's Leagues* (no covering letters). There was a detailed breakdown of age and participation by region in each of these surveys that I have not been able to reflect here due to contraints of time and space. As indicated in the main body of the work France has one of the largest and most improtant cohorts of female players in Europe with over 25,000 registered club-level participants by 1996. Women's football had been recognised since 1968 and given national association approval since 1970. The national first division had 12 clubs followed by a second tier of competition subdivided into 3 regional leagues of 10 clubs and a further 6 inter-regional leagues of 7 clubs. By 2003 there was one woman on the Council National du Football Amateur (CNFA) and twelve on the Commission Central Feminine (CCF). There was a national league of 12 clubs, a second regional tier of 3 groupings of 10 clubs, then six inter-regional leagues of seven clubs. These catered for around 28,065 players in total; all of whom were amateurs in 1997. By 2003 the number had grown to almost 35,000 players. At this time, the federation was concentrating on developing U21, U18 and U16 national squads, more youth comeptitions and a coaching pyramid. As one of the most important countries for women's football in modern times, a twenty-fifth anniversary international tournament was organised to mark the occasion in France. In 2003 Elisabeth Loisel was the women's national team head coach; Stéphanie Pilard the women's under 19 national team coach and Marilou Duringer a representative on the Federal Council for Women's Football. Elisabeth Loisel estimated a provisional budget of 500,000 Euros would be spent in the next few years to develop women's football in the country.

Georgia   *joined UEFA 1993 (N/R) 1996; 1997*

2003 FIFA questionnaire Circular 871 and *2003 UEFA Questionnaire on Domestic Women's Leagues* (no covering letters). Women's football was in its infancy in Georgia with some players joining clubs in Russia and Armenia. By 2003, coaching and development were a priority, though there were no dedicated staff for women's football. A development plan for girls and women's football was being developed. Maia Japaridze was a women's football instructor, as was Vladimir Panov.

Germany   *FR Germany and German DR joined UEFA 1954; the DFB and DVF combined as one national association following reunification in 1990.*

1996 UEFA Questionnaire; *1997 FIFA Survey Circular 609*; *2003 FIFA questionnaire Circular 871* and *2003 UEFA Questionnaire on Domestic Women's Leagues* (all anonymous, undated). As with the case of France, Denmark, England, and Norway, there was extensive additional information returned in the questionaire. As Germany is well-covered in the main body of this work, a brief summary of additional information will suffice here. Women's football in Germany started in 1970 and was recognised by the national association the same year, promoted by Willi Hink; Heike Ulriche and Hannelore Ratzeburg. At the 1980 conference on women's football, there were estimates of 110,000 women playing footbal in West Germany but it is unclear how many of these were registered players. FR Germany had 43,700 players in 1985, the highest number of registered players in Europe. Each of the 16 district associations of FR Germany was responsible for its championships, the winning teams would then play for the national championship which had been organised by the DFB since 1974. A Cup competition of the leading 15 teams had been organised since 1979. Each district has a representative team and indoor comeptitions. All female players were amateur. In the GDR there had been 50 teams in fifteen regular regional competitions, the winner of each would compete in a national championship. FSV Frankfurt was particularly noteworthy for its indoor, league, cup and other wins that year.

Teams Bundesliga Nord 95/6 and	**Bundesliga Sud 95/6**
Tennis Borussia Berlin	TUS Ahrbach
SV Grün Weiss Brauweiler	FSV Frankfurt
SG Rot Weiss Hillen	TSV Crailsheim
Turbine Potsdam	SC 07 Niederkirchen
FC Eintracht Rheine	SG Praunheim
PSV Rostock	VFR Saarbrücken
FC Rumeln Kaldenhausen	SC Klinge Seckach 1981 e.V.
TSV Siegen	VfL Sindelfingen
VfR Eintracht Wolfsburg	TuS Wörrstadt

By 2003, of an elite 500 women, playing at the top-level of the sport in Germany, 50 % were considered amateur, 49 % were semi professional and 1 % were professional. The main focus of the national association was to develop succesive generations of young women to sustain success in international competitons. Youth squads at Under 20, Under 18 and Under 16 national teams had been established. There were twenty-five women coaches who held the A license; 500 the B license and 6 the fussball-lehserin. The success of Germany at Women's World Cup in 2003 was condsidered to be due to this mentoring of both ex-national team players into coaching roles and young players.

2005 Fifth Women's Football Conference Oslo Norway 17-19 October 2005.

Giorgio Marchetti gave a presentation on UEFA's role in developing women's football. He suggested that the Women's Euro 2005 Final at Ewood Park between Germany and Norway set a new record with 21,100 fans in the stadium and a further 5.6 television viewers. Thr tournament averaged 7,800 spectators per match.

Willi Hink and Heike Ulrich gave a presentation entitled: «Women's Football in the Country of the World Cup and European Champions». By 2005 Gisela Gottringer was the Chair of the Girls' Football Committee; Willi Hink the Director for Women's Football, Amateur Football & Refereeing; Marit Stoppa Vice Chair of the Women's Football Committee; Tina Theune-Meyer a national team coach and Heike Ulrich head of the women's football department. They summarised the changing national association priorities as follows: from 1977 onwards the DFB sought to develop women in responsible positions; from 1982 participation in international competitions became more significant; in 1989 an advertising campaign for women's football was launched; from 1991 a competitive amateur league system took precedence. Since 2000, the national association sought to host more international competitions and events; develop clubs; extend pre-competition preparation periods and use former players for new jobs within the DFB. In 2003 investment in women's football increased to keep the strength of women's football in German domestic clubs and female players began to earn money with the national team. The Women's World Cup victory set television audience records at the ARD channel in Germany for women's sport. Around 10 million viewers, a market share of 33 % during regular match time, watched the Final. With highlights packages and multi-media replays, total viewing figures reached over 13 million Germans, comparable to a rating for a men's international match.

Greece   *joined UEFA 1954*

1996 UEFA Questionnaire; 1997 FIFA Survey Circular 609; 2003 FIFA questionnaire Circular 871 and *2003 UEFA Questionnaire on Domestic Women's Leagues* (all anonymous, undated). Women's football began experimentally in the 1980s, at the initiative of certain people in three or four women's clubs. The first few women's football clubs formed in 1987 and by the 1989-90 season the federation was organising a national championship between 15 teams in 3 groups. There was no separate women's association and Zissos Bellos had overall responsibility of the federation and was Chair of the committee overseeing the women's championships. There were no women on any committees in the national association. By 1997 there were 30 clubs in the national women's championships and another 10-15 which did not compete at this level, purely for financial reasons. There was stagnant growth for the next five years, due to the country's economic conditions. From a peak of 800 women players in 1997, the number descended, but since 2002 15 more clubs grew. Participation was most active in cities such as Athens, Thessalonika and larger towns. The season operated from the end of October and continues until the end of May.

In the national division, 12 teams played home and away ties; in the second division 18 teams competed in 3 regional groups, also in a home and away format. There were no national cup and no schools championships until 2003. Doxa Pireus won the league in 1997 and the other leading teams were: Artemis Pireus; A O Neapolt Athens; Ifestos Athens; AO Peristeri Athens; AO Egina; Olympiada Thessaloniki; AO Ilioupoli Thessaloniki; Olympiakos Kozani; Filyriakos Florina; Niki Kalamata and Rodopi Komotini. All female players were amateurs. There were two kinds of women's championships because of the geographical and economic situation; a Pan Hellenic competition of 10 teams at national level and a peripheral tournament of 3 groups comprising 6 teams. There were about 100 top-level women players in 1997 but plans for the Olympic Games provided a big impetus, as the host country was going to compete for the first time. There was one woman coach and thirty qualified referees.

UEFA Archive Records of 2002/4 Olympic and World Cup Competitions.

In 2002, a committee agreed the national teams who would take part in the women's football tournament at the Twenty-Eighth Olympic Games to be held in Athens 2004. It was agreed that female players must be at least 16 years old at the time of the tournament and that there was no upper age limit. These confederation berths were agreed as: AFC with 15 national associations was allocated 2 slots; CAF 14 associations 1 slot; CONCACAF 17 national associations 2 slots; CONMEBOL 7 national associations 1 slot; OFC 4 national associations 1 slot and UEFA 29 national associations 3 slots including Greece as host nation. Of the eighty-six women's national teams which enter preliminary competitions China PR; Japan; Nigeria; USA; Mexico; Brazil; Australia; Germany; Sweden and Greece comprise the ten women's finalists in Athens. Dimitrios Batsilas became the women's national team head coach; Sokratis Papadopoulos the technical committee chairman and Despina Papastathopoulou the women's football administrator.

Hungary *joined UEFA 1954 (N/R) 1996; 1997; FIFA
2003*

2003 UEFA Questionnaire on Domestic Women's Leagues (anonymous, undated). Women's football was in its infancy in Hungary with
some players joining clubs in Russia, Poland and Armenia. Women's
football was initially run by women until Hungarian FA took over in
2002. There were estimates of 34 teams with up to 700 women and
girls taking part in amateur competitions. A national championship was
planned for European competition preparation. By 2003, coaching and
development were a priority, though there were no dedicated staff for
women's football. There were no figures for referees or coaches. A
development plan for girls and women's football was being developed.
Andra Telek was women's national team head coach and Igaz András
the technical director.

Iceland *joined UEFA 1954*

1996 UEFA Questionnaire; *1997 FIFA Survey Circular 609*; *2003 FIFA
questionnaire Circular 871* and *2003 UEFA Questionnaire on Domestic Women's Leagues* all completed by Klara Bjamrtmarz, Secretary
Women's Committee of the FA of Iceland, Laugardal 104 Reykjavik
Iceland. Iceland has had women's football since 1972 and it was recognised by the national association the same year. In the 1996 season,
there were 8 teams in the top division and between 12 and 15 in the
second division. There were a total of 128 teams catering for the following number of players, categorised by age groups: Under 12, 1,925;
between the ages of 12 and 16 years old, 1,595; young adults aged
between 16-20, 448 and 617 adults. By 2003, there were approximately 4,300 amateur players, two-thirds of whom were aged nineteen or
over. There were around 30 women referees. There were two national
coaches, both female ex-players and several (up to fifty) at lower levels
in the game. There was a women's football committee but no separate
association. Elisabet Tomasdottir was on the board of the FA of Iceland
and Chaired the women's committee; Klara Bjartmarz was secretary of
women's committee; a further three women sat on that committee and
one on the technical board. The playing season started on the 20th May
and finished on the 15th December.

There were two divisions and 8 teams in the national first division. Five of the women's teams were from around Reykjavik; one was from the north of the island, another from Vestmann island, close to the south coast of Iceland, and eight from Akranes, about an hour's drive from Reykjavik. The second division was comprised 14 teams, subdivided into 3 regional groups and there was also a cup competition. The league winners for the last three years in a row had been Breidablik, the Milk Cup champions were Valur and the indoor champions Breidablik. The eight teams in the first division were Breidablik, Valur, IA, KR, Stjarnan, IBA, IBV and Afturelding. All female players were amateurs. There were senior, Under 20 and Under 16 national teams. There was one female coach, Vanda Sigurgeirsdottir for Breidablik. In addition, Arna Steinsen was the former coach of KR. Olafur Thor Gudbjornsson was the women's Under 19 national team head coach and women's football office manager.

Republic of Ireland   *joined UEFA 1954*

1996 UEFA Questionnaire; 1997 FIFA Survey Circular 609; 2003 FIFA questionnaire Circular 871 and *2003 UEFA Questionnaire on Domestic Women's Leagues* completed by secretary Pauline O'Shaughnessy Secretary of the Ladies Football Association of Ireland (LFAI). Ireland has had women's football since 1971 and has been recognised by the national association since 1973 as the Ladies Football Association of Ireland (LFAI). Charles Walsh had represented the Republic at the conference on women's football in 1980, when he had reported that there were fewer than 2,500 female players. There were 320 female teams registered with the Football Association of Ireland (FAI) by 1997. The President, Niamh O'Donoghue, was the LFAI representative on the national council; the international committee; the appeals; coaching and referees committees of the FAI. By 1997 there were 6,842 registered players of whom 3,325 were adult. The Schools Football Association oversaw developments in Irish Schools. There were no female certified coaches and 34 qualified referees. There was no national league until 2003, by which time participation had increased to over 10,000 women and girls. National team players were drawn from 300 Women's Football Association of Ireland (WFAI) teams, in 21 leagues throughout the nation, and the Irish diaspora. Noel King was appointed the women's national team coach in 2000 and a national under 19 and under 17 squad was developed under his guidance.

Israel   *joined UEFA 1994*

1996 UEFA Questionnaire; 1997 FIFA Survey Circular 609; 2003 FIFA questionnaire Circular 871 and *2003 UEFA Questionnaire on Domestic Women's Leagues* completed by Jacob Erel General Secretary of The Israel Football Assocation 12 February 1996 and then annonymously. There had been an international game against the Netherlands in 1977 and women's teams in the 1980s but women's football was not recognised by the national association in 1996. Women's football was recognised by the national association in 1997 and a national team established first, before regional clubs. Their largest defeat under the first coach, Rony Schneider, was to Poland in 1998, losing by thirteen goals to nil. By 2003 Alon Schaire had been appointed women's national coach and Haim Zimmer, the Israel Football Association (IFA) Chief Executive had overall control of the budget.

Italy   *joined UEFA 1954*

1996 UEFA Questionnaire completed with letter and enclosures from Marina Sbardella, President and Secretary of Women's Football Committee, 10 February 1996. Like France and Germany, the details of the enclosures were too extensive to incorporate here. There were 60 teams with 350 elite players in Serie A and B divisions plus a further 350 clubs in regional structures and approx 12,000 registered players. Marina Sbardella was President and secretary of the women's committee, supported by Fiorella Sciascia and Pina Debbi. There were 80 plus qualified women referees.

1997 FIFA Survey Circular 609 declined to respond by letter Fiorelli Sciascia 24/5/97.

2003 FIFA questionnaire Circular 871 and *2003 UEFA Questionnaire on Domestic Women's Leagues* (anonymous, undated). At the first conference on women's football Dr D Borgogno reported fewer than 2,500 women players in Italy. However, Italy were unofficial Euroepan champion in 1968 and ALFA unofficial world champions in 1981; 1984 and 1986. The second UEFA European Competition for National Women's Representative Teams final tournament was contested by Norway, Sweden, Italy and England in Norway during June 1987. In the third championship staged between 1987-9, 17 associations entered. Germany, Italy, Norway and Sweden qualified for final in Osnabruck Germany. Germany beat Norway 4-1 to become 1989 Champions with Italy again taking third place. Amongst the strongest European women's teams, Italy also lost in the UEFA European Finals in 1993 and 1997. The strongest teams in Serie A were Milan; Modena; Verona and Lazio. In 2000 former international player and leading goal scorer Carolin Morace was named head coach of the women's national team. She was succeded by Pietro Ghedin after she moved to coach the Canadian national women's team. By 2003, participation of over 10,000 women and girls was registered but not broken down by age groups. Elide Martini became women's national team administrator; Patrizia Recando the women's football division administrator and Alessandro Lulli the interpreter.

Kazhakhstan   *joined UEFA 2002*

2003 UEFA Questionnaire on Domestic Women's Leagues, (N/R).

Latvia   *joined UEFA 1992*

1996 UEFA Questionnaire completed by Voldemars Brauns, LFF General Secretary, 5 March 1996. There were 12 teams with 141 registered players of which 103 were in the 12-16 age group; 18 in the 16-20 band and 20 adults. There was no separate women's association and no women on the Executive Committee. The playing season ran from May to October and the top clubs included Fortuna (Ogre) who had two teams; Daugava; Kimikis; RAF; Dominante; Viksna; Varpa; Delfins; Osta; Solo and Jauniba. All female players were amateur. The national association took part in the annual Baltic Cup (Latvia, Lithuania, Estonia) since 1992 but were not yet ready to enter the Euro competitions yet.

1997 FIFA Survey Circular 609 completed by Voldemars Brauns, LFF General Secretary, 5 May 1997. Latvia has had women's football since 1986 and it was recognised by the national association in 1991. There were now a reduced number of players and teams, so the national association wanted to start school football but finance remained an issue. There were about 98 registered players in total: both adults and under 18s. There was one woman on the women's committee and one female coach but no referees. Newspapers such as Diena, Vakara Zinas and Riga Balss sometimes covered women's matches.

2003 FIFA questionnaire Circular 871 and *2003 UEFA Questionnaire on Domestic Women's Leagues* (undated and anonymous). Participation had increased to 250 women and girls helped by FIFA funding but finance remained an issue. The economic situation made youth development a priority. In 2003 Agris Bandolis became women's U19 national team head coach and Vilnis Klavins women's football manager. In spite of playing friendly international tournaments, the standard of play needed development. No referees or coaching courses had been planned but these were also priorities.

Liechtenstein   *joined UEFA 1974*

1996 UEFA Questionnaire; *1997 FIFA Survey Circular 609*003 FIFA questionnaire Circular 871 and *2003 UEFA Questionnaire on Domestic Women's Leagues* (undated and anonymous). The country has had women's football since 1985 and it was recognised by the national association the same year. There was a separate women's section and one person dedicated to female players. There were about 30 women players who were all classified as amateurs and 7 Under 15 participants. There was one woman coach. By 2003 there were 40 female players.

Lithuania   *joined UEFA 1992*

1996 UEFA Questionnaire; *1997 FIFA Survey Circular 609*; *2003 FIFA questionnaire Circular 871* and *2003 UEFA Questionnaire on Domestic Women's Leagues* (undated and anonymous). The country has had female football teams since 1994 and it was recognised by the national association the same year via a combined women's and youth committee. In 1996, development was overseen by the women's committee of the Lithuania Football Federation and there were two women on the Executive Committee. The season was played from the start of May to the end of October. There was one division of six teams. The League winner for that season was Kaunas Polytechnic women's team. All female players were amateurs. In 1994 Lithuania took part in the Euro competition for the first time. There were no female coaches or referees. Developments were hampered by a shortness of money but were promising. There were no women on any committees in 2003, three coaches and no referees. Lithuania co-organised the Baltic Countries Tournament with Latvia and Estonia. Rimas Viktoravicius was the women's national team head coach and Justina Lavrenovaite the women's football manager.

Luxembourg   *joined UEFA 1954*

1996 UEFA Questionnaire; 1997 FIFA Survey Circular 609; 2003 FIFA questionnaire Circular 871 and *2003 UEFA Questionnaire on Domestic Women's Leagues* (undated and anonymous). There was little interest but one team played in the German championship. Luxembourg has women's football since 1975, it was recognised by the national association the same year. There were fewer than ten adult teams in 1997, which had grown to 15 in 2003. Romain Jean was women's national team coach and Mick Loguercio national competitions secretary. Madame Chantal Berscheid had been on several FIFA refereeing courses.

FYR Macedonia   *joined UEFA 1994*

1996 UEFA Questionnaire and *1997 FIFA Survey Circular 609* responses from Ilija Atanasovsky General Secretary, Macedonian Football Union, Udarna Brigada, Republic of Macedonia 12 February 1996. There were no competitions for women or girls in 1996 and 1997.

2003 FIFA questionnaire Circular 871 and *2003 UEFA Questionnaire on Domestic Women's Leagues* (undated and anonymous). By 2003 there were 6-8 adult teams from which the national team were selected.

Dobrislay Dimoyski was the women's national team coach and Zlato Stojanoyski the women's football administrator. Priorities included youth football and more regional competitions.

Malta   *joined UEFA 1960*

1996 UEFA Questionnaire letter from Mrs Mary Micallef Secretary of the FA of Malta, 20 February 1996. There were 9 female teams with 141 registered players of which 43 were in the 12-16 year-old category; 15 in the 16 to 20 age band, plus 88 adults. There was a Chairman, Dr H Messina Ferrante, and a Secretary, Mrs Mary Micallef, in charge of female development. A seven-a-side league was played from February to the end of May each year and plans were in place to have a full-team league the following year. All female players were amateurs. There was no school football, no female coaches and no women referees.

1997 FIFA Survey Circular 609 (N/R).

2003 FIFA questionnaire Circular 871 and *2003 UEFA Questionnaire on Domestic Women's Leagues* (undated and anonymous). By 2003 there were ten adult teams from which the national team were selected and school football had begun.

Republic of Moldova   *joined UEFA 1994*

1996 UEFA Questionnaire letter from Pavel Ciobanu, General Secretary of the Moldavian FA, 15 February 1996. There had been no competitions since 1991 but the national association intended to start a championship with six teams next season.

1997 FIFA Survey Circular 609 anonymous, undated. The Republic has had women's football since 1989 and it was recognised by the national association since 1992. The difficulties of the transition period to Republic status had hampered growth. Moldova aimed to take part in the European championship and the Balkan Games in 1997. Valeriu Usatiuc, the Federal Inspector for women's football, was part of the national association but there were no women on committees. There was

a national amateur league in which 120 players participated (about half
of these were young players). The national team took part in friendly
matches in Lyon, France; Germany; Romania and the Ukraine. There
were two female coaches and two qualified referees.

2003 FIFA questionnaire Circular 871 and *2003 UEFA Questionnaire
on Domestic Women's Leagues* (undated and anonymous). By 2003
there were twelve adult teams from which the national squad was selected. Some players went to Russian teams and there were friendly
matches. Priorities included infrastructure and youth development.

The Netherlands   *joined UEFA 1954*

1996 UEFA Questionnaire letter from Mr Piet Hubers, the main contact
for women's football, 12 February 1996 and *1997 FIFA Survey Circular 609* anonymous, undated. The Netherlands had been present at the
1980 conference on women's football when it recorded the third largest European registration of female players (11,000), behind Denmark
(26,000) and West Germany (111,000). As one of the countries treated
in detail in the body of the book, this is a brief additional summary.
By 1997 there were 46,000 female registered players, compared with
950,000 male players. There were some 2,000 clubs, more than 75% of
which had only one team and many shared facilities with men's clubs.
Twelve clubs played in the national league. All regions played girls and
mixed football at under 12 and under 15 years of age but there were
no specific competitions for girls aged under 18. The development of
mixed football had led to a 25% increase in participation. There were
1,256 senior teams and 329 junior teams plus 516 at seven-a-side. One
woman sat on a district committee and one on the national board for
professional football. The football season for male and female players
ran from September to the end of May each year. There was one elite
league of 12 teams, two national leagues of 12 teams and nine further
district leagues. Female players were considered amateurs in all ways.
The responses were unclear on the number of female coaches and estimated that there were about 100 female referees. R Belksma-Konink
was an international FIFA-recognised referee. The Netherlands national association had organised a national symposium in 1997 to raise
awareness of women's football.

2003 FIFA questionnaire Circular 871 and *2003 UEFA Questionnaire on Domestic Women's Leagues* (undated and anonymous). By 2003 there were now over 60,000 women and 28,000 girls playing football. Since the introduction of mixed football this had expanded rapidly. The national football association oversaw all kinds of players. Joke Stig Rynbeek was the one woman on any of the committees. There was a national division of twelve teams; two divisions of 12 teams each plus numerous district leagues. Regional divisions had up to 1,300 teams. In the top national leagues there were 207 elite players but all were considered amateurs. The national team played in the Algarve Cup and the Nordic tournament. There were nine top-level; 6 mid-level and 30 lower-level female coaches. There were 90 plus qualified field referees and 58 indoor referees. There was only regional sponsorship, plus sponsors of the Dutch national team and the association.

Northern Ireland   *joined UEFA 1954*

1996 UEFA Questionnaire letter from David Bowen 15 March 1996; *1997 FIFA Survey Circular 609*; *2003 FIFA questionnaire Circular 871* and *2003 UEFA Questionnaire on Domestic Women's Leagues* (undated and anonymous). Women's football developed since 1976 after a meeting at the Post Office Youth Club, Belfast elected Mary McVeigh as Chair of the Northern Ireland Women's Football Association (NIWFA). Eighteen teams played in the inaugural season across three divisions. Honourary secretary, Maura Muldoon, oversaw developments and this was soon reduced to two divisions for ease of travel. A national league ran from April to August, plus three regional leagues with 8 teams in each. First division winners that year had been Belfast Amazons, while the Kilroot Strikers had won the second division. A national cup had been contested by the Belfast Amazons and the Carryduff Shield Ballymena All Stars. All female players were amateur. There were four qualified coaches but the national team was not strong enough for international participation. By 2003 almost 900 female players were registered in five divisions. All were amateur and a top priority was to develop the elite and grassroots elements of the game. Youth national squads were also targeted as important.

Norway   *joined UEFA 1954*

1996 UEFA Questionnaire anonymous, undated. The association placed a high priority on national teams with six full time talent–instructors for boys and girls equally. There had been a steady increase in playing numbers from 3,900 overall in 1990. In 1995, by age group, there were the following number of female players: Under 12, 1,800 clubs with 23,000 players in seven-a-side teams; in the 12-16 age-band 1,100 teams with 17,000 players; in the 16-20 age-band 146 teams for 2,400 players and at senior level 842 teams for 13,500 players. This gave a grand total of 3,984 teams with 55,500 players. Three of eight people on the FA Executive Committee were women. The season ran from mid-April to the end of October. The first division had 10 teams; there were six second divisions of 10 teams each and fourteen third divisions in which the number of teams varied. A further seven district divisions operated in areas with the highest activity around Oslo. SK Trondheims/Orn was the current holder of League Championship and IL Sandviken was the Cup winner. Clubs in the First division were Asker SK; Boler IF; Gjellerasen IL; SK Haugar; Klepp IL; Kolbotn IL; IL Sandviken; Setskog/ Holand FK; SK Sprint/ Jeloy and SK Trondheim/ Orn. All female players were considered amateurs but national team members may receive some financial support from the association. There were 240 qualified female referees.

1997 FIFA Survey Circular 609 anonymous undated. Norway has encouraged women's football since 1972 and it was recognised by the national association in 1976. There were 4,000 teams and close to 60,000 players, or about 1 in 5 players in Norway. All female players were considered amateur. Everyone at the association was responsible equally for men's and women's football. There were two full-time and 1.5 part-time posts to help development (supplementary information was provided here about players, leagues, coaches and developments, too extensive to include in this overview).

2003 FIFA questionnaire Circular 871 and *2003 UEFA Questionnaire on Domestic Women's Leagues* (undated and anonymous).

There were almost 65,000 registered players from under 12s to adult elite players. There was a first division for 10 teams at the elite level; a second division in 6 sections with 10 teams in each section; a third division of 10 teams in each section and a fourth, regional, division. Elite players had also competed in 18 matches at the Nordic Cup and Algarve Cup. Nine women held the highest-level coaching qualification; 37 at mid-level and there were 260 female referees. Up to 90 % of elite level matches were officiated by women. One exclusive sponsor promoted broad coverage of the national team. Co-organisers of the Algarve Cup in Portugal and Open Nordic Cup together with Portugal and Sweden in which 8 nations take part. By 2003 Karen Espelund, who had joined the Norwegian Football Federation at a young age, had become its first female General Secretary. Her influence on FIFA and UEFA committees was enormous. Norway remains the only country to have won FIFA women's World Cup, UEFA European and Olympic titles.

Poland   *joined UEFA 1954*

1996 UEFA Questionnaire; 1997 FIFA Survey Circular 609; 1996 UEFA Questionnaire and *1997 FIFA Survey Circular 609* all anonymous and undated. Poland has had women's football since 1981 when it played the first international game against Italy. Female participation became more encouraged by the national association in 1992 but economic problems had made growth slow. In this period, one of the strongest players was midfielder Maria Makowska, who became well-known while signed to Polish teams including Pafawag Wrocław and Stilon Gorzów in the national women's Ekstraliga. However, she moved to Germany, enjoying success with 1. FFC Turbine Potsdam until 2004. There were initially about 200 adult women players and the national association prioritised increasing the number of young women and girls. By 2003 over 900 participants were reported. The national association did not enter the UEFA women's comeptition until 1991 but has played in all UEFA competitions and FIFA World Cup qualifiers since then. No referees or coaches were mentioned. Makowska went on to play internationally for Poland in over 100 matches between 1986 and 2004.

Portugal   *joined UEFA 1954*

1996 UEFA Questionnaire and *1997 FIFA Survey Circular 609* both anonymous and undated. Portugal has had women's football since 1981/2 and it was recognised by the national association since 1993/4. There were initially about 600 adult women players and the national association prioritised increasing the number of young women and girls. Natália Castro headed up the women's committee, as there was no independent commission. There was a national championship for 14 teams. All female players were considered amateurs. 1.4% of coaches were women. There were no women referees. The national association also co-organised the Algarve Cup.

2003 FIFA questionnaire Circular 871 and *2003 UEFA Question-naire on Domestic Women's Leagues* anonymous, undated. Women's football was first played in 1980, there has been a national team since 1981 and league matches since the 1985/6 season. The most succesful women's clubs were Boavista FC; Gatoes FC and SU 10 Dezembro. There was an A national team, plus U19 and U18 squads playing 6 or 7 national games a season. No real TV coverage was reported. There were 110 licensed players under 16 and 1,297 adults plus some unli-censed participants, estimated at 345, in schools football. The season ran from June to July, playing in 42 amateur clubs and 15 seven-a-side teams, plus 16 squads in youth competitions. There was an amateur league knockout cup and seven-a-side competitions. Ana Caetano was secretary of the women's committee; Nuno Cristovao was the national team head coach and Monica Jorge was the assistant head coach.

Russia   *USSR joined UEFA 1954*

1996 UEFA Questionnaire and *1997 FIFA Survey Circular 609* both anonymous and undated. The Football Union of Russia has had wom-en's football since 1987 and female players were first recognised by the national association in 1989. Women's football teams were organised and played in the championship of the USSR until 1990. After the So-viet Union was disintegrated, some of the Russian-speaking popula-tion, moved to the other republics. Since then, the quality of play had improved but the number of teams had decreased because of financial problems. In the 1991-3; 1993-5 and 1995-7 rounds, Russia was the Group winner of their European Championship qualifying matches and in 1997 they made it to the Final tournament for the first time. The national association targeted Women's World Cup qualification as its top priority. The Association of Women's Football of Russia, with Oleg Lapshin as President, was incorporated into the Union. There were two women administrators: Olga Timofeeva (finance) and Raissa Alkina (Judicial). There was a Premier League with 12 teams. Regional competitions were held by Krasnoyarsk for 6 teams; Chouvashya for 4 teams; Voronezh for 6 teams and Ryazan for 4 teams. There were 32 women professional players; 180 semi-professional participants and 1,400 amateurs plus children: in all some 2,280 female players (sic). There was a national senior team, U18 and U16 squads. Between 1992 and 1996 the national team played 51 international matches and the U18 squad 14 fixtures. Olympic sports were generally favoured above football in schools. A Department for women's football had now been estblished in the Academy of Sports. There were three women coaches with midrange qualifications, plus 8 qualified referees and 12 assistants. There were no permanent sponsors.

2003 FIFA questionnaire Circular 871 and *2003 UEFA Questionnaire on Domestic Women's Leagues* anonymous, undated. Women's football had been part of the association activities since 1992. There were 24 U16 elite players and 378 adult players, with potentially 6,970 unlicensed players in total (the youth figure was not known). The season ran from April to October with five professional women's clubs; 12 amatuer adult clubs; 8 squads at U18 level and 8 youth clubs at U16 level in competitions. Since 1995 the age limit for mixed football has been 12 years old. There was a Russian National League Championship; a team championship; a Cup Championship of Russia; a Sports Day for Students and a Championship of Siberia. The best teams were Energia Voronezh; Moscow; Zvezda, SCK Samara, Rossiyanka and Lada Toliatti. There was a senior national team and an U19 squad. Around 6,500 viewers watched women's national team games per match and a total of 120,000 for league games per season. There were 73 league games of which 56 in the top division were televised. These had drawn a total of 66,750 and 54,750 live supporters respectively to the games. Not many national team games appeared on TV but highlights packages appeared on 7TV; NTV plus; Eurosport and local stations. Rosetel.com, Nike communications and sport equipment manufacturers sometime sponsor teams and individuals. Atovz cars sponsor Toliatti and Stavropol Energy provide some basic sponsorship. The national association wanted to develop chidren's football in regional competitions but no development plan is listed. An U17 WWC was a welcome suggestion, plus media events and promotions.

Romania   *joined UEFA 1954*

1996 UEFA Questionnaire and *1997 FIFA Survey Circular 609* completed by Christian Bivolaru, Secretary General 12 March 1997. Romania has had women's football since 1990 and it was recognised by the national association the same year. There were perhaps less than a hundred registered players. There had been a decreasing number since 1990, the problem was a lack of money in the economy generally. Mme Rodicia Siclovan was head of the women's commission within the national assocation. There were no further responses between 2.2 and 4.2 to this questionnaire.

2003 FIFA questionnaire Circular 871 and *2003 UEFA Questionnaire on Domestic Women's Leagues* anonymous, undated. Women's football in Romania has existed since 1990 and 145 licensed players were registered in 2002/3. There were no under 16 participants and unlicensed players were estimated at around 300. The season ran from September to June. There were six amateur clubs with no age-limit on mixed football. Knock out and league structures fed into a national team and U19 squads. The best teams were Motorul (Oradea); Fartec (Brasov); Conpet (Ploiesti) and Clujana (Cluj), who were the current champions. Around 100 league games had been noted and 300 national games had taken place. Some matches were broadcast on Realitatea TV, Antena 1. There was no main sponsor but Adidas provided some kit. The first participation of the U19 team in the 2002/3 championship was seen as a milestone. Mixed football for 8-13 year olds was encouraged. Of the 130 staff employed by the national association, there were 8 women including: Liana Stoicescu; Stefania Rasadeanu; Georghe Staicu; Maria Delicoiu (assistant national coach) and Luminita Camen (physiotherapist). The women's football committee had no development plan for women but there was one for girls, mixed football and women referees. The association recognised that 10% of FAP must be used for women's football, plus some of their own money.

Rep. of San Marino   joined UEFA 1988

1996 UEFA Questionnaire and *1997 FIFA Survey Circular 609* anonymous undated. There was no women's football. There were mixed «mini calcio» et «primi calci» small-sided games for 5 to 10 year olds. There were no further responses to this questionnaire.

2003 FIFA questionnaire Circular 871 (N/R) and *2003 UEFA Questionnaire on Domestic Women's Leagues* (N/R).

Scotland   joined UEFA 1954

1996 UEFA Questionnaire and *1997 FIFA Survey Circular 609* completed by Maureen McGonigle, Secretary of the Scottish Women's Football Association (SWFA). The SWFA was formed 1972 and affiliated to, but was not fully integrated with, the Scottish Football Association. From 1991, there had been 27 teams with 400 active players and 23 qualified coaches. Numbers had grown quickly by 1996 to 230 teams for 2,900 players and 2,074 qualified coaches. There was a senior league, with one national and three regional divisions. Of the 2,900 registered players, 800 were adults. All female players were amateur. Trips to Brazil had been organised and a triangular tournament took place betweeen Scotland, Northern Ireland and Wales. There were two Advanced-level and nine B-license coaches, plus 20 qualified referees.

2003 FIFA questionnaire Circular 871 and *2003 UEFA Questionnaire on Domestic Women's Leagues* anonymous, undated. Women's football had been organised by the national association since 1998 but a national team around since 1972. Under the age of 16 there were 1,500 players, plus 4,000 adults. Estimates suggested potentially 55,000 unlicensed players under 16 and the same number of adults. The season was played August to June. There were 40 amateur adult clubs and a further 30 youth teams subdivided into 3 leagues at U13/ U15/ U17 levels. The most important team was Kilmarnock (the sole answer given). There was a national team, an U19 and U17 squad, with about 15 overseas players from Australia, Norway, Denmark, Canada and the Netherlands playing at club level in the country. Some national team games were transmitted on Sky TV. The national association had the same kit sponsor as the men i.e Diadora and Fila. The women were also sponsored by Safeway supermarkets and the domestic league by Amicus, a Trade Union. Five female staff worked full time on women's football, most notably: Vera Pauw, coach and technical director; Sheila Begbie head of development and Maureen McGonigle, secretary of the Scottish Women's Football Association (SWFA). There was a women's section, not a committee. They have had a development plan since 1998. The respondee asked FIFA to lobby for more financial support for girls and women.

Serbia and Montenegro   *joined UEFA in 1954 as part of Yugoslavia as independent nations: Serbia rejoined UEFA in 2006 and Montenegro joined in 2007*

2003 FIFA questionnaire Circular 871 nd *2003 UEFA Questionnaire on Domestic Women's Leagues* anonymous, undated. The Football Association of Serbia and Montenegro was formed in 2003 and disbanded in 2006 by mutual consent. As former parts of Yugoslavia, the republics have organised women's football since 1972 and there was a national team since 1974. In 2003, there were estimates of 200 under 16 players and 200 adults plus a further 2,400 unlicensed participants in schools. All were amateur and there were 10 youth clubs in a league structure. The three top teams were Hasinac Classic WIS; Sloga Zehun and Yumco Vranje but there were no EU or overseas players in any of the clubs. There was an A national team, an U21 and U19. Some matches were televised on SOS Channel and All About Sport. The main sponsors were Yumco Vranje. A development plan was in place with Perica Krystic as head coach. There was a women's football committee, with specific targets of girls' football in school, an U16 national team by 2004 and an U14 national squad by 2006. The respondee asked for more financial support specifically for women's football.

Republic of Slovakia   joined UEFA 1994

1996 UEFA Questionnaire and *1997 FIFA Survey Circular 609* anonymous, undated. Women's football has existed since 1968 and was
integrated to the association the same year. The women's football
committee was part of the national association activities but no female administrators worked there. There were six female clubs which
played junior soccer, with 4 more such clubs planned. There was also
a national league in two groups with 14 elite teams overall. There were
885 female players, of which 407 were adults. All were considered
amateur. There were two coaches in the second (regional) category and
two without qualifications, plus two women referees.

2003 FIFA questionnaire Circular 871 and *2003 UEFA Questionnaire
on Domestic Women's Leagues* anonymous, undated. Since 1993 female players can get a licence to play as an adult at 15 years of age.
There were currently 359 registered participants under 16 and 632
adults, plus about 200 unregistered women and girls. The season was
played from July to June. There were 14 amateur clubs and 14 youth
clubs. Girls were involved from as young as 6 years of age, with no
age limit for mixed football until 1998, when it was fixed at the age of
15. There had been national and league matches since 1993. The three
best teams were Slovan Bratislava; MSK ZIAR Hronom and SKF VIX
Zilina with 2 or 3 players drafted in from the Czech Republic, Hungary
and the USA. STV1 transmitted some games on national television.
The main sponsors were Puma, Sportka and some individual firms.
There was no specific development plan and no specific staff for wom-
en's football.

Slovenia   joined UEFA 1994

1996 UEFA Questionnaire and *1997 FIFA Survey Circular 609*; *2003
FIFA questionnaire Circular 871* and *2003 UEFA Questionnaire on Domestic Women's Leagues* anonymous, undated letter from the Football
Association of Slovenia, Ljubjana. Women's football was incorporated
by the national association in 1990 with approximately 182 players under the age of 16; 182 adults and about 600 unlicensed participants. By
2003, there were 8 amateur senior clubs; 8 youth clubs and 40 schools

clubs. There had been 40 national team matches and league matches. The top teams were Ilirija Ljubljana; Skale Velenje and Krha Kovo Kesto. Overseas players from Croatia, Serbia and Montenegro sometimes played in these teams. There were U19 and U17 squads, in addition to the senior national team. The main aim of the association was the development of youth leagues and the existing five-year development plan estimated to spend 50,000 Euros to this effect. There were no employed women's football staff but there was a women's football committee comprised of female volunteers.

Spain   *joined UEFA 1954*

1996 UEFA Questionnaire and *1997 FIFA Survey Circular 609* completed by Teresa Andreau Grau, Presidenta Comité Nacional de Fútbol Femenino. Spain has had women's football since 1970 and it was integrated into the association's activities in 1980. There were a reported 2,497 players in 1992/3 and 7,500 in 1996/7. Teresa Andreau Grau was the President of the national committee for women and the main contact. There was a national league comprising 48 teams subdivided into 4 groups, plus several national cup competitions. There were 6,977 adult players and all were considered to be amateurs. There was one coach at level three (international); 58 at level 2 (regional) and 244 assistants (arbitras) in total.

2003 FIFA questionnaire Circular 871 and *2003 UEFA Questionnaire on Domestic Women's Leagues* anonymous, undated. Women's football has been played in Spain since 1981 and the national association took over in 1983. There have been 500 licensees since 1990 and the current figure was 9,217 players in 120 amateur clubs playing within a national league structure (with mixed football up to age 12). The best teams were Oroquieta Villaverde; Añorga KKE and Karbo. The TV station, Autonomicos sporadically showed games. There was no main sponsor but there were some regional arrangements such as supermarket sponsorship of local teams. There were development plans for a national league and no women in the administrative infrastructure of 105 people. There was a committee for women's football which was supporting many positive developments.

Sweden   *joined UEFA 1954*

1996 UEFA Questionnaire and *1997 FIFA Survey Circular 609* anonymous, undated. Sweden has been covered extensively in the main body
of the work so this is a very brief additional summary. Women's football
had been popular since 1968 and was integrated with the national association activities since 1970. At the conference on women's football
held in 1980, Sweden sent three respresentatives (T Brodd, G. Axels-
sen and R. Hernadi) who reported the fourth largest participation base
in Europe with 9,400 registered players. Sweden won the first UEFA
European competition for national teams by 4-3 in a penalty shoot out
with England in 1984. They were runners up to Norway in the 1989
competition and in the reached the semi finals in the third tournament.
The Swedish team finished sixth in the first Olympic finals and qualified for the European Championship in 1997. There was one woman on
the Executive Board and 13 on standing committees across the national
association. Pia Sundhage was mentioned as the main contact. There
was a national league for 12 teams, three second division groups of 10
teams and nine third division groups also with ten teams each. In addition there were district leagues of 4 and 5 teams. In total an estimated
95,000 girls and women played in Sweden broken down by age as:
60,000 under 16 years of age; 14,400 under 18 years old and 19,700
adults. There were five women coaches at the highest level; 9 qualified
referees in the first division and 20 more in lower leagues. The national
team was sponsored by national Lotto company, Svenska Spel.

2003 FIFA questionnaire Circular 871 included an extensive covering
letter, as did *2003 UEFA Questionnaire on Domestic Women's Leagues*
anonymous, undated. Women's World Cup 2003 was a big success.
Both the silver medal and the media coverage was important, when the
final against Germany was watched by 3.8 million people, almost half
the Swedish population. This closed a three-year project called Dam-
projektilen (translated as «Ladies project in» English) which had been
a big success. Women's football internationals had been around since
1973 when Sweden first played agains Finland and there had been a
national team since then. Players were licensed at the age of 15 years.
Therefore player numbers, broken down by age group were: 60,000
participants under 16 in 2003 and 39,730 adults, in addition to unli-

censed players. The season ran from April to November and there was mixed football since 1996. Some players were semi professional in the twelve elite clubs; there were an additional 2,000 amateur and 7,000 youth clubs. Competitions included a national league, a cup comeptition, regional league structures for semi pro and amateur players, plus the Swedish Championship for Futsal five-a-side. The eight-team Algarve Cup in Portugal was an important regional competition in which Sweden and Norway took part, as was the Open Nordic Cup. The Open Nordic Club Championship was co-organised between Finland, Norway, Sweden and Denmark.

The best teams in Sweden were Alvsjo AIK; Nalmu77 Umeå IK and Sitex/ Utaback. Ten to fifteen overseas players were signed in the elite teams, from Finland, Norway, USA, England and Poland. There was a national team plus U21; U19 and U17 squads. Attendance at home national games was about 29,000 spectators and league totals for all games 92,000 supporters (across 132 league games). Women's games were sometimes shown on TV 4, 1 on SVT 24 and SVT 1. Betting and the lottery, Svenska Spel, were the main sponsors. Aftonbladet was the main newspaper coverage and 3 telecom companies (not named) also provided sponsorship. Equipment providers included Adidas, Puma, Nike and Umbro, plus regional sponsors. The big development had been focused on the national team and youth teams, plus a «ladies project» for women leaders. The national association had spent eleven million Swedish Krona, equating to 1.25 million Euro between 1999-2003 on various projects. Of 90 administrative staff 10 were women including Markia Mominski Lyfors (National coach); Anne Signeul (coach U19); Annelie Gustafsson (U17); Nils Andersson and Cecilia Sanders. Pia Sundhage had moved from being Head Coach of the Boston Breakers in the WUSA professional league to become head of the USA women's national team. The defeat to Germany in the Final of the Women's World Cup 2003 broke new domestic television records for women's football. The game was watched live on television by 4 million viewers; with an average of 3.2 million during regular time rising to 3.8 million in extra time. This was the highest audience rating by the channel for any programme that year. Sweden had therefore easily qualified for the 2004 Olympic comeptition. The respondee asked FIFA for a Women's Football Development Committee with five-year plans and would welcome more meetings on the issue.

Switzerland   *joined UEFA 1954*

1996 UEFA Questionnaire and *1997 FIFA Survey Circular 609* completed by the Secretary of the FA, undated. The Swiss FA has recognised women's football since 1970 under, the ZUS (amateur league)
control. Activities were more thoroughly integrated to the SFV association in 1993 with estimates of between 3,000 and 6,000 players. There
was a national division for 10 teams; a second division of 10 teams;
plus there were regional leagues with 2 groups of 10. Further district
leagues in groups of ten provided comeptition for around 110 junior
clubs. There were estimated a total of 250 teams. All female players
were amateur and 87% of Swiss players were adults. There were 4 A-
licence, 13 B-licence and 86 C-licence women coaches. There were 5
qualified female referees and 10 assistants.

2003 FIFA questionnaire Circular 871 2003 and *2003 UEFA Questionnaire on Domestic Women's Leagues* anonymous, undated. There has
been a Swiss national team since 1970 and the national assocation took
over women's football in 1993. There were a reported 5,000 Under 16
licensed players and 8,500 adults. There were estimates of a further
30,000 unlicesed youth participants and 30,000 adults. The season ran
from August to June for 200 adult amateur clubs and 200 clubs for
under 15 players. The best clubs were Bern; Sursee; Schwerzenbach
and Seebach. Some Italian players competed in Swiss clubs at elite
levels but the respondant was not sure whether they did so as professionals. There was a senior national team and U19 and U17 squads.
There was no official sponsor. The national association had a development plan for women's football, including developing the under 17
national team further, and it had invested about Swiss FR 700,000.
The women's football administrators were Betrice von Siebenthal and
Marcello Cuccuzza as Chair and Secretary of the committee respectively. The women's committee also had a development plan for a national team talent identification project. The respondee asked FIFA for
an U17 World Cup for women, an Under 19 development symposium
and more media promotion.

Turkey   *joined UEFA 1955*

1996 UEFA Questionnaire; *1997 FIFA Survey Circular 609*; *1996 UEFA Questionnaire*; *1997 FIFA Survey Circular 609* and 2003 UEFA Questionnaire on Domestic Women's League all anonymous and un-dated. Turkey has had women's football since 1989 when students played the game in colleges. Female participation became more en-couraged by the national association in 1992 but economic problems had made growth slow. There were initially about 200 adult women players and the first national league was created in the 1993 season for five clubs, mostly around Istanbul. The national association priori-tised increasing the number of young women and girls, adding more regional competitions in 2003. Over 500 participants were reported in 34 clubs, including some youth competitions. The national association wanted to develop Under 17 and Under 15 national squads in order to compete in the UEFA and FIFA comeptitions for women's football. No coaches or referees were mentioned.

Ukraine   *joined UEFA 1993*

1996 UEFA Questionnaire and *1997 FIFA Survey Circular 609* com-pleted by Sergei Karcharov Chair of women's football committee. Ukraine has supported women's football since 1988 and it was in-tegrated to the association activities in 1991. However, the unstable and precarious economic set-up adversley affected the promotion of women's football. The number of sides fell from 24 to 7 in 1997, with maybe 600 women still active as players. All were amateur.

2003 FIFA questionnaire Circular 871 and 2003 UEFA Questionnaire on Domestic Women's League anonymous, undated. There had been a national team in Ukraine since 1993 but there was no national league. The season was played from April to November for 10 amateur adult clubs and 10 youth teams. The total number of players was given as 150 under 16 years of age and 300 licensed adults. Estimates of unli-censed players ran to 800 under 16 participants and 400 adults. Since 2002 Ukraine had hosted The Leather Ball Cup, an Under-14 mixed-event. The most successful teams were «Donchanka» from Donetsk; «Legenda» from Charnigov and «FC Kharkiv» from Kharkiv. The latter were the 2003 champions. Between 1999-2000 there had been fifteen foreign players including those from Russia, Georgia, Armenia and Azerbaijan. Then, in 2000/1 ten overseas players from Russia, Moldova and Belarus played in Ukraine; decreasing to eight the next season. There had been six overseas players in 2003 from the same three countries. The national association had launched the All-Ukraine Programme of football development in Ukraine 2003-8. This five-year plan includes women in management and administration. There were no women in decision-making bodies but there was, for example, a Finance Director, Head of International Licensing and several administrators. There were also plans for female coach licensing and admittance to universities. Six female referees had been included in the plans for international competitions. There was a women's football committee. Since 2000, the national association had hosted more regional competitions, plus 4% of FIFA funding had been given to football classes in schools and the association for women's football. This had totalled US$ 100,000 by the Football Federation of Ukraine for the development of women's football in clubs. There were no main sponsors of the women's league but plants, factories and private companies did offer some financial support. The All-Ukraine fund for the Development of Music, Culture and Sports had also contributed along with some Lotto funding. There was limited TV coverage on First National and regional stations. There was currently no national league but plans to develop regional competition. There was no discrete development plan for girls football. The respondee asked FIFA for more media coverage, including an award for the best female player in the world.

Wales   *joined UEFA 1954*

1996 UEFA Questionnaire and *1997 FIFA Survey Circular 609* anonymous, undated. Wales has had women's football since 1972 and it has been integrated at association level since 1992. The country was represented at the conference on women's football in 1980 by Mr T. Morris who reported participation under 2,500 women and girls. There followed a significant increase in the five years between 1992 and 1997, with a national development-team and the first schools junior female tournament. The women's coordinator was Helen Croft and David Collins was Seretary General of the association. There were no female

professional players; up to 1,000 adult amateurs and 800 girls reportedly involved.

2003 FIFA questionnaire Circular 871 and 2003 UEFA Questionnaire
on Domestic Women's League anonymous, undated. There were a total of 17 staff in the national football organisation (FAW) and none
were dedicated solely to the development of women's football. Coaching and youth development were the national association priorities.
There were no sponsors. There was no development plan for girls and
women's football. Press coverage was occasional and there was little
television interest. There was an official league and a national team
which had played matches since 1993. The national association had
not had funding to enter UEFA and FIFA competitions until 1997. The
most succesful teams were Cardiff Ladies; Newport Strikers and Ban-
gor City. Many of the better players became involved at universities
and colleges. No foreign players were currently active in Wales. There
was a senior national team and an Under 19 team. Andrew Beattie was
the women's football manager and Gillian Kozak the competition administrator. The season ran from August to May in which 30 senior
clubs and 20 youth clubs competed; further subdivided at U12 and U16
levels. It was estmiated that there were a further 600 under 16 non-
licensed players and 300 adults active. Priorities were a national league
and regional structures to encourage more youth players.

Yugoslavia   *joined UEFA 1954*

1997 FIFA Survey Circular 609 anonymous, undated. Yugoslavia
had women's football since 1969 and the activity was integrated to
the association activities on 15 July 1972. A commission for women's
football oversaw an A league (of 8 clubs) and a B league (of 6 clubs)
comprising 209 players. Of this total, 20% of female players were considered professional; 30% semi professional and 50% amateur. With
the Yugoslav wars of the 1990s, this development spread across the
newly independent nations summarised in this appendix.

Appendix 4: How UEFA has grown: newly affiliated full members since 1954

1954	Albania	German DR	Poland	(30 members)
	Austria	Greece	Portugal	
	Belgium	Hungary	Romania	
	Bulgaria	Iceland	Scotland	
	Czechoslovakia	Ireland Republic	Spain	
	Denmark	Italy	Sweden	
	England	Luxembourg	Switzerland	
	Finland	Netherlands	U.S.S.R.	
	France	Northern Ireland	Wales	
	FR Germany	Norway	Yugoslavia	
1955	Turkey			(31 members)
1960	Malta			(32 members)
1964	Cyprus			(33 members)
1974	Liechtenstein			(34 members)
1988	San Marino			(35 members)
1990	Faroe Islands			(36 members)
1992	Estonia	Latvia	Lithuania	(38 members)*
1993	Armenia	Belarus	Croatia	(44 members)
	Georgia	Slovenia	Ukraine	
1994	Azerbaijan	Israel	Macedonia	(49 members)
	Moldova	Slovakia		
1996	Andorra			(50 members)
1998	Bosnia and Herzeg.			(51 members)
2002	Kazakhstan			(52 members)

* After the reunification of Germany

References

Abrams, N., 2005: «Inhibited but not ‹crowded out›: The Strange Fate of Soccer in the United States», *International Journal of the History of Sport*, 12 (3): 1-17.

Adderley, J., 2006: «Women's Football», *BBC Nation on Film*, London: BBC.

Adidas promotional leaflet, 1999: *FIFA Women's World Cup 1999*, Los Angeles.

Agergaard, S. and Bothelo, V., 2010: «Female Football Migration: Motivational Factors for Early Migratory Processes», in Maguire, J. and Falcous, M. (eds), *Sport and Migration: Borders, Boundaries and Crossings*:157-172.

Andrews, D., Pitter, R., Zwick, D. and Ambrose, D., 1997: «Soccer's Racial Frontier: Sport and the Suburbanisation of Contemporary America», in Armstrong, G. and Giulianotti, R. (eds), *Entering the Field: New Perspectives on World Football*: 261-283.

Aldis, C., 2001: *British University Sports Association: Women's Football files 1980-1999*.

Anderson, B., 1991: *Imagined Communities*, New York: Verso.

Anonymous, 1895: «Ladies football», *Penny Illustrated*, 23 February.

—,1895: «The Ladies' Football Club», *Daily Graphic*, 25 January.

—,1917: «Personal Column», *The Times Tuesday*, December 18.

—,1921: «Should Women Play football?», *Table Talk*, 28 July.

—,1921: «English Girl Teams Play Football for Charity», *Pawtucket Times*, 9 September.

—,1983: «Women's football in ancient China», *National Women's Soccer Invitational Brochure*, Beijing China.

Anthony, D., 1970: «When to kick is unwomanly», *Times Educational Supplement*, 10 October.

Armstrong, G. and Guilianotti, R. (eds), 1997: *Entering the Field: New Perspectives on World Football*, Oxford: Berg.

Austad, R., 2010: Røa IL Team Manager Response to Questionnaire, 13 May.

Bairner, A., 2001: *Sport, Nationalism, and Globalization. Europe and North American Perspectives*, Albany: SUNY Press.

Bale, J., 1979: *The Development of Soccer as a Participant and Spectator Sport: Geographical Aspects,* London: Sports Council/Social Science Research Council.

—,1980a: «Women's Football in England and Wales: a Social-Geographic perspective», *Physical Education Review,* 3 (2): 20-34.

—,1980b: «The Adoption of football in Europe: an Historical-Geographic Perspective», *Canadian Journal of History of Sport and Physical Education,* 11 (2): 40-52.

Bale, J. and Maguire, J. (eds), 1994: *The Global Sports Arena: Athletic Talent Migration in an Interdependent World,* London: Frank Cass.

Banet-Weiser, S., 1999: «Hoop Dreams: Professional Basketball and the Politics of Race and Gender», *Journal of Sport and Social,* 23 (4): 324-431.

Batt, P., 1973: «Dates have the order of the boot», *The Sun,* 17 April.

Battersby, K., 1994: «Mohr earns Germany first leg advantage», *Daily Telegraph,* 2 December.

Begbie, S., 1996: «The Story So Far: Recent Developments in Women's Football in Scotland», *Scottish Journal of Physical Education,* 24: 44-48.

Bennett, A., 2004: *The History Boys,* London: Faber and Faber.

Besson, R., Poli, R., & Ravenel, L., 2011: *Demographic Study of Footballers in Europe 2011,* Neuchâtel: CIES.

Bethell, A., 1983c: *Gregory's Girl,* Cambridge: Cambridge University Press.

Beveridge, S., 1975: «Edna - The Sad Soccer Star», *Sunday People,* 31 January.

Bhattacharya, N., 1992: *Hem and Football,* London: Secker and Warburg.

Blatter, J., 2010: «President's Corner», *FIFA World: For the Game, For the World*: 27

—,2006: «Promising Preparations for WWC 2007», *FIFA News,* 19 March.

—,1995: «The Future is Feminine», «FIFA News», July.

—,1984: *General Secretary FIFA Circular 338 to all associations,* 22 June, Zurich: FIFA.

Boaler, J., 1994: «When do Girls Prefer Football to Fashion?», *British Educational Research Journal,* 20 (5): 46-60.

Bourke, W., 2000: *Daughter of Alice Mills Lambert, essays, newspaper cuttings and eulogy provided by personal communication,* 23 June.

Bouzanquet, J.-F., 2009: *Fast Ladies: Female Racing Drivers 1888-1970,* Dorchester: Veloce.

Boyle, R. and Haynes, R., 2004: *Football in the New Media Age,* London: Routledge.

Brand, A. and Niemann, A., 2007: «Europeanisation in the Societal/Trans-National Realm: What European Integration Studies Can get Out of Analyzing Football», *Journal of Contemporary European Research,* 3 (3): 182-201.

Brennan, P., 2007: *The Munitionettes: A History of Women's Football in North East England During the Great War,* Donmouth: Donmouth Publishing.

Brown, A., 2000: «European Football and the European Union: Governance, Participation and Social Cohesion-Towards a Policy Research Agenda», *Soccer and Society,* 1 (2): 129-150.

Brownell, S., 1995: *Training the Body for China: Sport and the Moral Order of the People's Republic,* Chicago, Illinois and London: University of Chicago Press.

Burke, P., 2005: «Patriot Games: Women's Football during the First World War in Australia», *Football Studies,* 8 (2): 5-19.

Carroll, S., 1999: «The Disempowerment of the Gender Gap: Soccer Moms and the 1996 Elections», *Political Science and Politics,* 32 (1): 7-11.

Caudwell, J., 1999: «Women's Football in the United Kingdom: Theorising Gender and Unpacking the Butch Lesbian Image», *Journal of Sport and Social Issues,* 23 (4): 390-403.

—,2002: «Women's experiences of sexuality within football contexts: A particular and located footballing epistemology», *Football Studies,* 5 (1): 24-45.

Chang, W., 1981: *President ROCFA «Welcome Speech» World Women's Invitational Tournament 1981 Taipei,* 11 October.

Charlton, B., 1969: *Bobby Charlton's Book of European Football,* London: Souvenir Press Ltd.

—, 2007: *My Manchester United Years: The Autobiography,* London: Headline.

Chastain, B., 2004: *It's Not About the Bra: Play Hard, Play Fair, and Put the Fun Back Into Competitive Sports,* New York: Harper Collins.

China PR Football Association, 1991: *Football in China: Present Problems and Future Prospects,* 16 November, Zurich: FIFA Archive.

—,1991: *China '91: 1st FIFA World Championship for Women's Football for the M&M's Cup,* Zurich: FIFA Archive.

Chye Hin, T., 1981: *Vice President ALFC «Re: Women's Football in Asia»,* 28th October 1981, Correspondence File, Zurich: FIFA Archive.

Close, P., Askew, D. and Xu, X., 2006: *The Beijing Olympiad: The Political Economy of a Sporting Mega - Event,* London and New York: Routledge.

Collins, S., 2006: «National Sports and Other Myths: The Failure of US Soccer», *Soccer and Society,* 7 (2-3): 353-363.

Corinthians (Manchester), 1951: *Corinthian v Lancashire Ladies Programme,* Festival of Britain Craven Park 21 July.

—,1952: *Corinthian versus Bolton Programme, Manchester Athletic Ground,* 20 August.

Cox, M., 2011: «Gaining Acceptance», *FIFA World,* March.

Crolley, L. and Hand, D., 2006: *Football and European Identity: Historical Narratives Through the Press,* London: Routledge.

Cubberley, H., 1932: «Soccer for Girls», *Spaldings Athletic Library-Soccer for Women.*

Davis, J. and Brewer, J., 1992: «Physiological characteristics of an International Female Soccer Squad», *Journal of Sports Science,* 10 (3): 142-143.

—,1993: «Applied Physiology of Female Soccer Players», *Sports Medicine,* 16 (2); 180-189.

Davies, H., 2004: *Boots, Balls and Haircuts,* London: Octopus Publishing.

Davies, P., 1996: *I Lost My Heart to The Belles,* London: Mandarin.

De Longevialle, A., 2009: *La Construction de L'Europe du football,* PhD thesis, University of Strasbourg.

Deloitte, 2008: *Annual Review of Football Finance 2008,* London: Deloitte.

Dhami, N., 2011: *Katy's Real Life: The Beautiful Game Series,* London: Orchard.

Dietschy, P., 2010: *Histoire du Football,* Paris: Librairie Académique Perrin.

Dine, P. and Crosson, S. (eds), 2010: *Sport, Representation and Evolving Identities in Europe,* Bern: Peter Lang.

Duke, V. and Crolley, L., 1996: *Football, Nationality and the State,* London: Longman.

Duret, S., 2011: «First Ladies», *FIFA World,* April.

Edelman, R., 1993: *Serious Fun: A History of Spectator Sport in the USSR,* New York: Oxford University Press.

Drevon, A., 2005: *Alice Milliat: La Pasionaria du Sport Feminine,* Paris: Vuibert.

Eisenberg, C., Lanfranchi, P., Mason, T. and Wahl, A., 2004: *100 Years of Football: The FIFA Centennial Book,* London: Weidenfeld and Nicholson.

European Commission Communication, 1996: *Incorporating Equal Opportunities for Women and Men into all Community Policies and Activities,* Section 67, Luxembourg: Office for Official Publications of the European Communities.

—,1998: *Incorporating Equal Opportunities for Women and Men into all Community Policies and Activities,* Luxembourg: Office for Official Publications of the European Communities.

—,2001: *Towards a Community Strategy on Gender Equality (2001-2005),* Luxembourg: Office for Official Publications of the European Communities.

Allatt, C., 1988: *Analysis of questionnaire with reference to the interest shown in girls in full time education in the playing of Association Football 19 September,* English Schools FA.

Equal Opportunities Commission, 1978: *The Football Association Limited and Nottinghamshire Football Association v Miss T Bennett,* Transcript of Judgement, 28 July.

—,1999: *Hardwick, Vs the FA Employment Appeal Tribunal,* Transcript of Judgement, 30 April.

Espelund, K., 1995: *Developing Women's Football,* UEFA Youth Conference Paper.

Fasting, K., 2004: «Small Country Big Results: Women's Football in Norway», in Fan Hong and Mangan, J.A., *Soccer Women and Liberation Kicking Off a New Era,* 149-162.

FIFA, 1973: *Minutes of the First UEFA Women's Football Conference 22 March,* Zurich: FIFA Archive.

—,1974a: *Letter from Dr H Käser to Mr T Croker,* 17 January, Correspondence File, Zurich: FIFA Archive.

—,1974b: *Letter from H Käser Secretary to Pat Gregory,* 20 June, Correspondence File, Zurich: FIFA Archive.

—,1980: *Minutes of the Second UEFA Women's Football Conference,* 19 February, Zurich: FIFA Archive.

—,1981: *Minutes of the meeting of the 1981 FIFA Technical Committee Item 1 Women's football and competitions. Discussed by Group A,* 17/18 December (Zurich), Zurich: FIFA Archive.

—,1984: *Walter Gagg FIFA. Proposition pour l'organisation d'un tournoi mondial de football féminin pour équipes representatives,* Correspondence File, Zurich: FIFA Archive.

—,1985: *Willy Simonsen Norges Fotballforbund, Item 4,* 30 December (Oslo), Correspondence File, Zurich: FIFA Archive.

—,1986a: *Minutes of Meeting with Peter Verlappan, General Secretary AFC,* 17 April, Zurich: FIFA Archive.

—,1986b: *Minutes of the 45th Ordinary Congress,* 29 May (Mexico City), Correspondence File, Zurich: FIFA Archive.

—,1988: *Minutes of the 46th Ordinary Congress,* 2 July, Zurich: FIFA Archive.

—,1991: *China '91: First FIFA World Championship for Women's Football for the M&M's Cup FIFA,* Zurich: FIFA Archive.

—,1992: *1st FIFA/ M&Ms Symposium on Women's Football November,* Zurich: FIFA Archive.

—,1997a: *Survey of Women's Football Zurich January,* Zurich: FIFA Archive.

—,1997b: *Committee for Women's Football Minutes of Meeting No.10,* 18 February, Zurich: FIFA Archive.

—,1998: *Evaluation of the Questionnaire on Women's Football as at 30.7.97,* 2 March, Zurich: FIFA Archive.

—,1999: *2nd Symposium on Women's Football,* 8 July (Los Angeles), Los Angeles: Hilton and Towers.

—,2000: *Minutes Meeting Number 6 of the Organising Committee for the Olympic Football Tournaments,* 27 September (Sydney), Zurich: FIFA Archive.

—,2002: *Minutes Meeting Number 2 of the Organising Committee for the Olympic Football Tournaments,* 29 October (Zurich), Zurich: FIFA Archive.

—,2006: *FIFA Big Count 2006: 270 million people active in football,* [www.fifa.com/aboutfifa/media, accessed November 2010].

—,2010: *EXCO Summary,* Zurich: FIFA.

Fishwick, N., 1989: *English Football and Society: 1910-1950,* Manchester: Manchester University Press.

Foulds, S. and Harris, P., 1979: *America's Soccer Heritage,* Manhattan Beach (California): Soccer for Americans.

Gehrmann, S., 1997 (ed), *Football and Regional Identity in Europe,* Münster: Lit Verlag.

George, S. and Bache, I., 2001: *Politics in the European Union,* Oxford: Oxford University Press.

Gibson, A. and Pickford, W. (eds), 1906: *Association Football and The Men Who Made It,* London: Caxton Publishing.

Giulianotti, R. and Robertson, R., 2009: *Globalization and Football,* London: Sage.

Glanville, B., 1973: «Goals and Gals don't really mix», *The Sunday Times,* 24 June.

—,1980: *The Story of the World Cup,* London and Boston: Faber and Faber Ltd.

Goldblatt, D., 2007: *The Ball is Round,* New York: Penguin

Gregg, L., 1999: *The Champion Within: Training for Excellence,* Burlington: JTC Sports.

Gundle, S., 2008: *Glamour: A history,* Oxford: Oxford University Press

Hall, M. A., 2003: «The Game of Choice: Girls' and Women's soccer in Canada», *Soccer and Society,* 4 (2-3): 30-46.

Hamm, M., 2004: *With Carol Thompson Winners Never Quit!,* New York: Byron Press Visual Publications.

—,1999: *Go For the Goal: A Champion's Guide To Winning In Soccer And Life,* New York: Harper.

Hardy, S., 1986: «Entrepreneurs, Organizations and the Sports Marketplace: Subjects in Search of Historians», *Journal of Sport History,* 13 (1): 14-33.

—,1997: «Entrepreneurs, Organizations and the Sports Marketplace», in Pope, S. W. (ed), *The New American Sport History: Recent Approaches and Perspectives,* 14-33.

Harris, J., 2001: «Playing the man's game: Sites of resistance and incorporation in women's football», *World Leisure,* 43: 22-29.

—,2005: «The Image Problem in Women's Football», *Journal of Sport and Social Issues,* 29 (2): 184-197.

Harvey, A., 2005: *Football: The First Hundred Years, The Untold Story,* New York and London: Routledge.

Havelange, J., 1991: *China '91: 1st FIFA World Championship for Women's Football for the M&M's Cup,* Zurich: FIFA Archive.

Hennies, R., 1995: «Firm Bases - Scope at the Summit?», *FIFA Magazine,* May.

Henry, J. and Comeaux, H., 1999: «Gender Egalitarianism in Coed Sport: A Case Study of American Soccer», *International Review For the Sociology of Sport,* 34 (3): 277-290.

Highfield Oral History Group and the Sir Norman Chester Centre for Football, 1993: *Highfield Rangers Highfield Rangers: an Oral History,* Leicester: Leicester City Council Living History Unit.

Hill, Jeffrey and Williams, J. (eds), 1996: *Sport and Identity in the North of England,* Keele: Keele University Press.

Hill, J., 2010: «Postmodernism and the Cultural Turn», *Sport in Modern Europe: Perspectives on a Comparative Cultural History,* Symposium One, [www.sport-in-europe.group.cam.ac.uk/symposium1summaries. htm, accessed 10 March 2011].

Hink, W., 2009: *DFB Response to FIFA Questionnaire on Women's Football,* 23 September.

Hobsbawm, E., 1990: *Nations and Nationalism Since 1870: Programme, Myth, Reality,* Cambridge: Cambridge University Press.

Hobsbawm, E. and Ranger, T. (eds), 1992: *The Invention of Tradition,* Cambridge: Cambridge University Press, 1992.

Hoffmann, E. and Nendza, J., 2006: *Verlacht, Verboten und Gefeiert: Zur Geschichte des Frauenfußballs in Deutschland,* Weilerwist: Landpresse.

Holt, R. and Mason, T., 2000: *Sport in Britain 1945-2000,* London: Blackwell.

Hong, F. and Mangan, J. A. (eds), 2003: *Soccer, Women and Sexual Liberation: Kicking Off a New Era,* London: Frank Cass.

House of Commons Select Committee, 2006a: *Second Special Report: Women's Football Department for Culture, Media and Sport,* 25 July.

—,2006b: *Fourth Report of Session 2005-06: Responses from the Department for Culture, Media and Sport, the Football Association and the Football Foundation,* 19 October.

International Olympic Committee, 2000: *The Promotion of Women in the Olympic Movement,* Lausanne: Department of International Co-operation.

—,2005: *IOC Report Women participation at the Games of the XXVIIIE Olympiad Athens 2004 Dept of International Co-operation and Competition,* February.

—,2006: *Women in the Olympic Movement - Women in Sport Leadership Evaluation of the 10%-20% Objectives,* Department of International Cooperation and Development, November.

ITN Source, 1957a: «Women's Football in Stuttgart», Pathé, 1 January, BP010157149729

—,1957b: «Britain beat Germany 4-0 in European Championship in Berlin», Pathé, 1 January, BGY502140342.

—,1957c: «Germany and United Kingdom ends with draw», Pathé, 1-15 August, BP050857149724.

—,1958: «Millions take a breather», Pathé, 1 January, BP010158154511.

—,1959: «Football's A Girl's Game», Pathé, 12 July, BP020759158729.

—,1960: «The First International Show Girls Soccer Tournament Brazil», 10 August, BGY503290098.

—,1975: «Eire: Woman footballer to play in Belgium's Leading Ladies Team», 14 January, BGY509180617.

Jarvie, G., 2003: «Internationalism and Sport in the Making of Nations», *Identities: Global Studies in Culture and Power,* 10 (4): 537-551.

Jacobs, B., 2004: *Dick Kerr's Ladies*, London: Constable and Robinson.

Jensen, E., 2011: *Body by Weimar: Athletes Gender and German Modernity*, Oxford: Oxford University Press.

Jinxia, D., 2002: «Ascending then Descending? Women's Soccer in Modern China», *Soccer and Society*, 3 (2): 1-18.

Käser, H., 1980: *letter Re: Women's Football / The Olympic Games to Pat Gregory,* Women's Football Association England, dated 17 June private collection.

Kassimeris, C., 2010: *Football Comes Home: Symbolic Identities in European Football*, London: Lexington Books.

Keys, B., 2006: *Globalizing Sports: National Rivalry And International Community in the 1930s*, Boston: Harvard University Press.

King, A., 2003: *The European Ritual: Football in the New Europe*, Aldershot: Ashgate.

Knoppers, A. and Anthonissen, A., 2003: «Women's Soccer in the United States and The Netherlands: Differences and Similarities in Regimes of Inequalities», *Sociology of Sport Journal,* 20 (4): 19-37.

Korr, C., 1986: *West Ham United: The Making of a Football Club*, Michigan: University of Illinois Press.

Kowalski, R. and Dilwyn, P., 1997: «Political Football: Moscow Dynamo in Britain, 1945», *International Journal of the History of Sport*, 14 (2): 100-121.

Kunz, M., 2010: «The Female Figure: Vital Statistics From the Women's Game», *FIFA World*, March.

Kuper, S., 1994: *Football Against the Enemy*, London: Orion Books.

Lanfranchi, P., 1994: «Exporting Football: Notes on the Development of Football in Europe», in Giulianotti, R. and Williams, J. (eds), *Game Without Frontiers: Football, Identity and Modernity*, 163-172.

Lanfranchi, P. and Taylor, M., 2001: *Moving with the Ball: The Migration of Professional Footballers*, Oxford: Berg.

Leigh, M. and Bonin, T., 1977: «The pioneering role of Madame Alice Milliat and the FSFI in establishing international trade for women», *Journal of Sport History*, 4 (1): 72-83.

Leenders, T., 1991: *China '91: 1st FIFA World Championship for Women's Football for the M&M's Cup*, Zurich: FIFA Archive.

Levermore, R., 2010: «CSR for Development Through Sport: Examining its Potential and Limitations», *Third World Quarterly*, 31 (2): 223-241.

Liston, K. and Booth, S., 2010: «The Atlantic Drift: Preliminary Empirical and Theoretical Observations», *Sport as a Global Labour Market: Female Football Migration Research Workshop*, University of Copenhagen, 2-3 December.

Longman, J., 2001: *The Girls of Summer: The U.S. Women's Soccer Team and How It Changed the World*, New York: Harper Paperbacks.

Lopez, S., 1997: *Women on the Ball: A Guide to Women's Football*, London: Scarlet.

Marschik, M., 1998: «Offside: The Development of Women's Football in Austria», *Football Studies*, 1 (2): 69-88.

Markovits, A. and Hellerman, S., 2003: «Women's Soccer in the United States: Yet Another American Exceptionalism», in Fang Hong and Mangan, J.A. (eds), *Soccer, Women and Sexual Liberation: Kicking Off a New Era*, 14-30.

Mason, T., 1980: *Association Football and English Society 1863-1915*, Brighton: Harvester.

Melling, A., 1998: «Cultural Differentiation, Shared Aspiration: The Entente Cordiale of International Ladies' Football 1920-45», *The European Sports History Review*, 1: 27-53.

—,1999: *Ladies Football: Gender and Socialisation of Women Football Players in Lancashire 1926-1960*, PhD thesis, University of Central Lancashire.

—,2001: «Charging Amazons and Fair Invaders: The Dick Kerr's Ladies Soccer Tour of North America of 1922 - Sowing Seed», *European Sports History Review*, 3: 155 - 180.

Mennesson, C. and Clement, J., 2003: «Homosociability and Homosexuality: The Case of Soccer Played by Women», *International Review for the Sociology of Sport*, 38 (3): 311-330.

Munting, R., 2007: «Norwich Girls' Football in the inter-war years», *Bulletin of the British Society for Sports History*, March: 8-15.

Myotin, E., 1999: *Sports Socialisation of 11-20 year old Brazilian girls in the 1990s: A Social Psychological Study*, PhD thesis, University of Loughborough.

National Football Museum, 2011: *Hall of Fame Inductees*, [www.nationalfootballmuseum.com/halloffame, accessed 10 January 2011].

Neale, W. C., 1964: «The Peculiar Economics of Professional Sports», *The Quarterly Journal of Economics*, 78 (1): 1-14.

Nelson, M. B., 1996: *The Stronger Women Get, The More Men Love Football: Sexism and the Culture of Sport*, London: Women's Press.

Newsham, G., 1998: *In A League of their Own*, London: Scarlet.

Owen, W., 2005: *Kicking Against Tradition: A Career in Women's Football*, London: Tempus.

Pannick, D., 1983: *Sex Discrimination in Sport*, London: Equal Opportunities.

Parillo, B., 1999: «Women's World Cup 1999», *Providence Journal*, 10 May.

Parrish, R., 2003: *Sports Law and Policy in the European Union*, Manchester: Manchester University Press.

Pauw, V., 1999: «From Wishful Thinking to Development Policy», *Second FIFA Women's Symposium*, Los Angeles.

Pielichaty, H., 2009: *Do Goalkeepers Wear Tiaras Too?*, London: Walker.

Polley, M., 2004: «Sport and National Identity in Contemporary England», in Smith, A. and Porter, D. (eds), *Sport and National Identity in The Post War World*: 22-23.

Poli, R., Ravenel, L. and Besson, R., 2010: *Annual Review of the European Football Player's Labour Market 2010*, Neuchatel: CIES.

Porter, D., 2004: «Your boys took one hell of a beating! English football and British decline, c.1950-80», in Smith, A. and Porter, D. (eds), *Sport and National Identity in the Post-war World*, 31-51.

Prudhomme-Poncet, L., 2003: *Histoire du Football Feminin au XXe Siècle: Espaces et Temps du Sport*, Paris: L'Harmattan.

Richards, J., 2001: «Our Kelly», *Total Football Magazine*, July.

Robertson, R., 1992: *Globalization: Social Theory and Global Culture*, London: Sage.

Ronan, S., 2011: *Soccer Sisters: FA of Ireland*, KISS Workshop presentation, 24 February (Nyon: UEFA HQ).

Rottenberg, S., 1956: «The Baseball Players' Labor Market», *The Journal of Political Economy*, 64 (3): 242-258.

Russell, D., 1997: *Football and the English: A Social History of Association Football in England, 1863-1995*, Preston: Carnegie.

Schwules Museum, 2011: *Celebrating the Women's World Cup 2011*, [www.schwulesmuseum.de, accessed 1 April 2011].

Scraton, S., Fasting, K., Pfister, G. and Vazquez, B., 1998: «Women and Football – A Contradiction? The Beginnings of Women's Football in Four European Countries», *The European Sports History Review*, 1: 3-9.

Scraton, S., Cauldwell, J. and Holland, S., 2005: «Bend it Like Patel, Centring ‹Race›, Ethnicity and Gender in Feminist Analysis of Women's Football in England», *International Review for the Sociology of Sport*, 40 (1): 71-88.

Sloane, P. J., 1971: «The Economics of Professional Football: The Football Club as a Utility Maximiser», *Scottish Journal of Political Economy*, 18 (2): 121–146.

Simonton, D., 1998: *A History of European Women's Work, 1700 to the Present*, London: Routledge.

—,2011: *Women in European Culture and Society: Gender, Skill and Identity from 1700*, London and New York: Routledge.

Sky Sports, 2011: «Emma Byrne: Away From the Game», *Sky Sports*, April/ May.

Talbot, M., 2000: *Gendering the Sport Agenda in Sport Decision Making European Women and Sport*, Conference 6/8 July, Helsinki.

Taylor, M., 2005: *The Leaguers: The Making of Professional Football in England 1900–1939*, Liverpool: Liverpool University Press.

—,2006: «Global players? Football Migration and Globalization 1930-2000», *Historical Social Research*, 31 (1): 7-30.

—,2008: *The Association Game: A History of British Football 1863-2000*, London: Longmans/Pearson.

—,2010: «Football's Engineers? British Football Coaches, Migration and Intercultural Transfer, c1910-c1950s», *Sport in History*, 30 (1): 138-163.

The Football Association, 1969: *Minutes of the FA Council,* Item 37, 1 December.

—,1970: *Minutes of the FA Executive Committee*, item 16, 16 December.

—,1971: *Minutes of the FA Executive Committee*, item 46, 19 January.

—,1974: *Minutes Joint Consultative Committee for Women's Football,* Lancaster, 3 October.

—,1997: *Women's Football Alliance Minutes, Appendix D,* 21 November.

—,2001: «Developing Asian Girls Football», *On the Ball*, London: The FA.

The Football Favourite, 1921: «The New Beauty and the Beast», 26 February: 8.

Timisela, F., 2011: «Fien Timisela Profile», *Dutch Soccer Academy in the United States*, [www.dutchsocceracademy.com/coaches, accessed 2 April 2011].

Tischler, M., 1981: *Footballers and Businessmen: The Origins of Professional Football in England*, New York: Homes & Meyer.

Turner, G. and Idorn, J., 2004: *UEFA: 50 Years*, Nyon: UEFA.

UEFA, 1973: *Minutes of Meeting on Women's Football, 21 March (Zurich),* Nyon: UEFA Archive.

—,1980: *Minutes of the Second UEFA Women's Football Conference,* 19 February, Zurich: FIFA Archive.

—,1981: *Minutes of Conference on Women's Football,* 17 March (Lisbon), Nyon: UEFA Archive.

—,1982: *Minutes of UEFA Committee on Women's Football,* 31 March (Zurich), Nyon: UEFA Archive.

—,1984: *UEFA Minutes Committee on Women's Football,* 10 July (Geneva), Nyon: UEFA Archive.

—,1994: *Working Group on Women's Football,* 23 May (Dublin), Nyon: UEFA Archive.

—,1998: *Third Women's Conference on Women's Football,* London, Nyon: UEFA Archive.

—,2000: *Women's Committee Minutes*, Nyon: UEFA Archive.

—,2001/2- 2008/9: UEFA Women's Cup Regulations, Nyon: UEFA Archive.

—,2001a: *Fourth Conference on Women's Football (Oberhausen)*, Nyon: UEFA Archive.

—,2001b: *Minutes of Coaches Round-Table Discussion with Women's National Team Coaches*, Nyon: UEFA Archive.

—,2003: *Questionnaire on Domestic Women's Leagues*, Nyon: UEFA Archive.

—,2004: *First Elite Coaches Forum*, Nyon: UEFA Archive.

—,2005: *Fifth Conference on Women's Football, Oslo*, Nyon: UEFA Archive.

—,2006: *Second Elite Coaches Forum (Nyon)*, Nyon: UEFA Archive.

—,2007a: *Third Elite Coaches Forum (Nyon)*, Nyon: UEFA Archive.

—,2007b: *Training Ground: Woody and Wulfy Showboat in Bilbao*, [www.uefa.com/trainingground/skills/, accessed 10 January 2012].

—,2009a: *Women's Champions League Regulations 2009/10*, Nyon: UEFA Archive.

—,2009b: *First UEFA Women's National Team Coaches Conference*, Nyon: UEFA Archive.

—,2010/1: *UEFA Financial Report 2010/11*, Nyon: UEFA.

UEFA EXCO, 2010: 0*69: UEFA Executive Committee decisions from Prague meeting*, [www.uefa.com/uefa/mediaservices/mediareleases, accessed 20 December 2010].

V&A Museum, 2009: *The Cold War and Modern Design 1945-1970*, London: V&A, [www.vam.ac.uk/exhibitions/future_exhibs/cold_war, accessed 1 April 2010].

Wagg, S., 1984: *The Football World: A Contemporary Social History*, Brighton: Harvester.

—, 2007: «If you want the girl next door...»: Olympic Sport and the Popular Press in Early Cold War Britain», in Wagg, S. and Andrews, D. (eds), *East Plays West: Sport and the Cold War*, London and New York: Routledge.

Walvin, J., 1994: *The People's Game: The History of Football Revisited*, Edinburgh; London: Mainstream Publishing Co.

Whitehead, L., 2007: *Women's Professional Soccer: A Comparative analysis between the Top domestic leagues in Denmark, England and Germany and the Women's LLC League in the USA*, MBA Football Industry thesis, University of Liverpool.

WFA Correspondence File, 1973: *P. Gregory to Dr H Käser Secretary FIFA*, 20 July.

—,1974: *P. Gregory to Dr H Käser Secretary FIFA*, 2 June.

Williams, J., 2003: *A Game for Rough Girls: A History of Women's Football in England*, Oxon: Routledge.

—,2007: *A Beautiful Game: International Perspectives on Women's Football*, London: Berg.

Williamson, D., 1991: *The Belles of the Ball*, Devon: R & D Associates.

Woodhouse, D., 2001: *The Post War Development of Football for Females: A Cross Cultural and Comparative Study of England, The USA and Norway,* PhD thesis, University of Leicester.

Yates, C., and Vassilli, P., 2011: «Moving the Goalposts: History of Women's Football in Britain Exhibition (1881-2011)», *The Peoples History Museum*, Manchester, 15 March 2011, [http://www.footballfineart.com, accessed 12 April 2011].

Zhenqi, Q., 1982: «Women's Soccer has a Bright Future», *National Women's Soccer Invitational Brochure*, Zurich: FIFA Archive.

CENTRE
INTERNATIONAL
D'ÉTUDE DU SPORT

Savoirs sportifs
Collection dirigée par Denis Oswald et Raffaele Poli

Ouvrages parus

Droit

Denis Oswald, Associations, fondations, et autres formes de personnes morales au service du sport, XXXVI, 371 p., (vol. 2) 2010.

Sciences sociales

Raffaele Poli, Le marché des footballeurs. Réseaux et circuits dans l'économie globale, 180 p., (vol. 1) 2010.

Monica Aceti & Christophe Jaccoud (éd.), Sportives dans leur genre ? Permanences et variations des constructions genrées dans les engagements corporels et sportifs, 182 p., (vol. 3) 2012.

R. Poli, J. Berthoud, T. Busset & B. Kaya (éd.), Football et intégration. Les clubs de migrants albanais et portugais en Suisse, 162 p., (vol. 4) 2012.

Jean Williams, Globalising Women's Football. Migration and Professionalization, 183 p., (vol. 5) 2013.